Praise for
NOT IN IT TO WIN IT

For as long as I've known Andy Stanley, he has championed the primacy of reaching people as the task of the church. As he often says (quoting James, a first-century leader of the church), "We ought not make it hard for the gentiles who are turning to God." I believe the issues Andy raises in this book are the most pressing questions facing the church right now, and they get at the heart of the Great Commission itself. I invite you to wrestle with them thoughtfully and prayerfully, as I have. If we are to represent Jesus in this generation, we must be people full of grace and truth, and that is no small challenge. Even in places where you come to different conclusions than Andy, you'll be richer for having wrestled through these issues.

J. D. GREEAR, pastor of The Summit Church

Andy is "not in it to win it," and I'm in it with Andy and his passion for reaching people far from Jesus. Too many Christians are fighting the wrong battle and warring against the wrong people—you can't wage war on people and reach them at the same time. Andy points us back to the mission Jesus sent us on—showing the love of Jesus to a broken and hurting world. This book is a prophetic call to a confused church, and I hope it is widely engaged and discussed.

ED STETZER, dean and professor at Wheaton College

As someone who studies and serves churches around the world, I can confirm it. Attendance in churches is declining. Fewer people, especially in the younger generations, identify as Christians. Churches are more divided than ever. Our world seems more divided than ever. By any measure, we are not winning. But what if we're not winning primarily because we're trying to win? Once again, Andy Stanley helps us reflect on the words of Jesus and challenges us to consider a better way to live our lives and, more importantly, engage God's mission in a broken world.

TONY MORGAN, founder and lead strategist of The Unstuck Group, author of *The Unstuck Church*

NOT
IN IT
TO
WIN IT

NOT
IN IT
TO
WIN IT

WHY CHOOSING SIDES
SIDELINES THE CHURCH

ANDY STANLEY

ZONDERVAN
REFLECTIVE

ZONDERVAN REFLECTIVE

Not in It to Win It
Copyright © 2022 by Andy Stanley

Requests for information should be addressed to:
Zondervan, *3900 Sparks Dr. SE, Grand Rapids, Michigan 49546*

Zondervan titles may be purchased in bulk for educational, business, fundraising, or sales promotional use. For information, please email SpecialMarkets@Zondervan.com.

ISBN 978-0-310-13892-1 (softcover)

ISBN 978-0-310-13894-5 (audio)

ISBN 978-0-310-13893-8 (ebook)

Cover design: Brand Navigation
Interior design: Kait Lamphere

To pastors who refuse to politicize the church and have chosen instead to lead their congregations through the current political and cultural crisis with clarity, boldness, and grace. Press on!

CONTENTS

Acknowledgments xi

Introduction: Unprecedented xv

PART 1: MY 2020

1. Battle of the Buckets 3
2. Culture War Christianity 19
3. Canceled 35

PART 2: OUR HISTORY

4. Kingdoms in Conflict 61
5. On Brand 76
6. One for the Win 106
7. The Supper of God 123
8. Inquisitor in Chief 146

PART 3: THE WAY FORWARD

9. Apply Only as Directed 171
10. Most Important Now 197

Notes 219

About the Author 230

ACKNOWLEDGMENTS

To the fabulous, mission centered, Jesus following people who serve, support, and attend our network of churches in the greater Atlanta area, thank you! The past two and half years have been challenging for pastors everywhere—especially for those who, because of their commitment to making disciples of people in all parties, refused to politicize their churches. While I navigated my fair share of pressure to "chose a side" and "take a stand," that sentiment paled in comparison to the avalanche of encouragement I received from you to stay the course—your calls, letters, voicemails, DMs, emails, and notes left in our mailbox at home. You'll never know how much your support in this season meant to Sandra and me. I've said it before, but I don't say it enough: I'm convinced you are the most mature, forward leaning, Jesus focused congregation in America, which means I'm the most blessed pastor anywhere. These past two and a half years have confirmed that conviction.

When I committed to writing *Not in It to Win It*, one of the first people I called was Ruth Malhotra. I've known

Ruth and her family for many years. Ruth's response was, "Oh my! Are you sure you want to do this?" I assured her I did, but not without her help. She agreed and poured countless hours into research, chapter drafts, the development of illustrations, and dozens of "Are you sure you want to say that?" As grateful as I am for Ruth's editorial partnership, I am grateful to Ruth for another reason as well. She agreed to take on this project during what she considers the most stressful season of her life. On several occasions I gave her an off-ramp to allow her to focus on personal and professional issues that would have more than consumed the average person. But anyone who knows Ruth knows there's nothing average about her. Thank you, Ruth!

This project would never have gotten to the finish line without the focus, attention to detail, and energy of Suzy Gray. But Suzy brought more than her professionalism to this project. Her passion for the topic of this book was inspiring and instructive. And at times, irritating. Who would have the nerve to tell a seasoned author, not to mention one's employer, "I think you should cut that entire chapter. It causes the book to lose momentum." Suzy Gray, that's who. And she was right. And so I did. Suzy, thank you for consistently telling me what I need to hear even when you know I won't want to hear it. Everybody who knows you knows you make everything better.

On the publishing side, I'm so grateful once again to my friends at Zondervan. Ryan Pazdur, John Raymond, and Jesse Hillman in particular. Ryan, a special shout-out to you is in order. Your editorial and content advice on this project was extremely helpful in light of the subject matter. Beyond that, I sensed genuine passion regarding the messaging and overall impact of this project. Thank you!

Last but first. Sandra. When I told you I felt compelled to weigh in on this topic, you smiled and said, "Okay, if you're sure." Which I took to mean, "If you're going there, I'm going with you."

Other than me, only you know the crazy that gravitates in our direction when I step out to address concerns we both agree need to be addressed. No one feels the weight of the criticism that comes my way like you do. You carry it well, with dignity and grace. How many times have you taken my hand and said, "If they knew you, they wouldn't say things like that about you." The best decision of my life was asking you to marry me. Everyone who knows you agrees.

INTRODUCTION

UNPRECEDENTED

2020

A pandemic that created an
economic shutdown that left us
teetering on financial meltdown
while navigating social unrest
during an election year.

It was my first time.

Yours too.

No instructions, mentors, or maps. We were on our own.
But we weren't alone.

Those of us in leadership felt the weight of responsibility in ways most of us were unprepared for. People were looking to us for even a morsel of clarity amid demoralizing uncertainty.

I certainly felt that pressure. I felt it as a parent, a pastor, and an employer.

The year 2020 brought out the best and the worst in us. It exposed weaknesses and showcased strengths. It slowed us down in some arenas and forced us to speed up to keep up in others. According to Scott Galloway, author of *Post Corona: From Crisis to Opportunity*, the pandemic was an accelerant. "Take any trend—social, business, or personal—and fast-forward ten years."[1]

No wonder we were exhausted.

Throughout 2020 I encouraged the folks in our congregations to *write a pandemic story they would be proud to tell*. I would ask, "When 2020 is nothing but a story you tell, what story do you want to tell? A story of panic, fear, selfishness? Or a story of faith, compassion, fidelity, generosity?" I would remind them, "You're writing your pandemic story one decision and one response at a time. Write a good one!"

Sadly, many evangelicals did *not* write a good one.

DISCOVERY ZONE

When life is predictable, it's natural to lose sight of what we value most, what we fear most. But when a tsunami of uncertainty rolls in, things get real, real quick. Uncertainty doesn't alter our value system. It exposes it. Without any effort on our part, what's *really* most important surfaces immediately. In seasons of uncertainty, we discover what we value most. Uncertainty and the fear that follows close behind strip away the veneer and reveal what's hidden beneath the surface.

In 2020 evangelicals in America discovered what we

value most. The political, social, economic, and health crises of 2020 didn't cause us to misprioritize our values. These events simply exposed what's been true for a long time. While our *actions* don't always tell the whole story, our *reactions* most certainly do. The reactions of prominent pastors, Christian podcasters, television personalities, and nonprofit leaders to the events that defined 2020 revealed the disturbing reality lurking beneath Bible-laced rhetoric, faith claims, books, music, and sermons for a long time. Turns out what we say is most important is not actually what we consider most important.

Our responses to 2020 made that abundantly clear. Even worse, our responses to the events of 2020 made our values *embarrassingly* clear.

People were watching.

Listening.

Consequently, folks who don't embrace our faith discovered what's most important to us as well. And while *we* may be surprised by what 2020 revealed about us, they aren't. They suspected it all along. Our response to the events of 2020 simply confirmed their suspicions—namely, that once you scratch off the veneer of our sermons and songs, we value what everybody else does.

And what does the evangelical church in America value most?

Winning.

What do we fear?

Losing.

Not winning or losing souls. We systematically alien-
ated more than half the souls in America through our un-
Christlike rhetoric and fear-based posturing. For all our
talk of evangelism, revival, and reaching the lost, clearly
those are not our primary concerns. That's not what we
value most. If it were, we would not have allowed ourselves
to be dragged into and embroiled in far less noble conflicts
with far less noble goals. If evangelism and discipleship
were truly most important, we would not have so easily
surrendered influence with those who need to be evange-
lized and discipled. We would not have allowed ourselves
to be reduced to a voting bloc. A constituency. Part of the
electorate. Pawns.

Tragically, because of our misplaced, un-Christlike
value system . . . our love affair with winning . . . we were
not prepared or positioned to take advantage of what, in
hindsight, may have been the greatest opportunity for the
church in our lifetime—an opportunity when, to borrow
the apostle Paul's words, we had a chance to *shine* like stars
in the heavens, to live like "children of God without fault in
a warped and crooked generation."[2] Instead, to use Paul's
words again, we *grumbled* and *argued*. With one another.
With our neighbors. With state and local governments. To
use Jesus's words, we had an opportunity to let our "light
shine before others, that they may see your good deeds and
glorify your Father in heaven."[3]

Instead, we hid our light under a bushel. We lined up
behind our political party of choice and leveraged our sacred

text to validate our political talking points. We argued with our brothers and sisters and treated our neighbors with suspicion. We went to war with state and local officials over our *right to gather* . . . shoulder to shoulder . . . indoors . . . in the middle of a pandemic. We left the impression that our personal faith would suffer irreversible harm if we couldn't meet indoors every seven days. On social media we demonized and criticized, by name, people we'd never met. We gave up the moral high ground and confirmed what my kids' generation has suspected for some time—namely, we don't actually believe what we claim to believe. Our rhetoric and our responses say otherwise.

We allowed ourselves to be divided over masks and vaccines. Perhaps the apex of the insanity being that not an insignificant number of evangelical Christian leaders considered—and still consider—COVID vaccines the *mark of the beast.*

I'm still looking for the beast.

Indiscriminate demonization of entire people groups was considered an exercise in virtue. After all, we were standing up for the truth!

We would not be intimidated!

We were fighting the good fight.

We were in it to *win* it!

Toward the end of 2020, as the prospects of winning politically and culturally began to slip away, many high-profile evangelical church leaders behaved as rudely and as un-Christlike as their secular counterparts. In some instances, worse. In their attempt to save America from the other political party, they lost their opportunity to save half the American population from their sin. Consequently, we all lost influence. We all lost credibility.

Then the candidate backed by the majority of evangelicals lost the election.

PRONOUNS

If you're confused or offended by my use of a collective *we*, I get it. After all, we've never met, so what right do I have to assume you took part in or condoned any of this? And doesn't *we* include me?

Yes.

I've chosen my pronoun on purpose because if you're a Jesus follower, you are included in *we*. And you are a part of *we* because *we* are one—one body united by one Savior and one baptism. I may not know you, but I can't do without you. You may not like me, but you need me and are connected to me. The apostle Paul thought so anyway. When Paul used the body analogy to describe the highly dysfunctional church in Corinth, he did not give anyone the choice to opt out. He did just the opposite: "Now you *are* the body of Christ, and each one of you *is* a part of it."[4]

Implication: You're all one whether you like it or not and whether you like one another or not.

They were a *we*.

And so are we.

As much as I would like to differentiate and distance myself from the behavior of some parts of the body, I can't. And neither can you. And that's okay, considering what else Paul wrote about this uncomfortable arrangement: "God has put the body together, giving greater honor to the parts that lacked it, so that there should be no division in the body."[5]

Who put us together?

According to Paul, God did. And he did it so that there would be . . . wait for it . . . *no division*. Like your physical body, each part of the church body "should have *equal concern* for each other. If one part suffers, every part suffers with it."[6]

So there's no room for you versus me. Like it or not, like me or not, there's just *we*. If you sprain your ankle, the other parts of your body don't look the other way or post about your ankle on social media. They don't blame; they engage. They come to the rescue. When one part of your physical body suffers, the entire body suffers.

So this is a *we* problem. And *we* must address it.

The problem I'm referring to—the Achilles' heel in modern evangelicalism—is our obsession with winning. It's a fatal weakness because even a cursory reading of the Gospels and the letters of Paul make one thing abundantly clear. The church is not here to win. Just the opposite. By every human measure, our Savior *lost.*

On purpose.

With a purpose.

And *we* are his body.

So, like our Savior, we are not in it to win it. We are in it for something else entirely.

That something else is what this book is about.

PART ONE

MY 2020

CHAPTER ONE

BATTLE OF THE BUCKETS

Difference is inevitable. Division is a choice.

Our nation chose poorly.

The church followed suit.

In our current cultural climate, there are no neutral topics or neutral people. Everything and everybody is politicized and forced to fit neatly into one of two buckets.

A red one or a blue one.

This isn't new. Political polarization has been a national reality for decades. But during 2020, the messy but often productive middle ground all but disappeared. As a result, Americans were pressured to move further right or further left or be left behind.

Lines were drawn where lines were deemed unnecessary in the past.

Everything became a point of contention. School closings. School openings. Masks. Protests. And, of course, Anthony Fauci. Republicans loved him. Then Democrats claimed him.

With the collapse of the middle, nuance left the building.

Without nuance, comments are taken more literally than intended, and productive discussion around complex topics becomes virtually impossible. The result: you're for me or you're against me. It's all or nothing. But every adult knows the world doesn't work that way. Nothing works that way. That way of thinking ensures that things *won't* work.

But, as every political pundit knows, "all or nothing" sells. "All or nothing" gets votes. It's a donation magnet. A brand builder.

People should know better. Christians in particular.

Unfortunately, and to the point of this book, churches, church leaders, and prominent pastors (along with high-profile leaders of faith-based organizations) took their cues from culture and vacated the middle. To our shame they added their voices to those of their secular counterparts. Not wanting to be left out—and certainly not left behind—we entered the partisan fray. We did what everyone else was doing, pretty much the way they were doing it. We sided publicly with a party and a candidate—and defended both regardless.

In short, we forgot what it means to be Christian.

In the first century, *Christian* was a political term, not a religious one. First-century followers of Jesus weren't branded Christian to differentiate them from Zeusians or Jupiterians. The term *Christian* was coined based on Latin political terminology. Christian was analogous to other political associations such as *Caesariani*, a follower of Caesar; *Herodiani*, a follower of Herod; or later,

Neroniani, a follower of Nero.[1] Non-Christians in Antioch, where the term *Christian* was first coined, viewed followers of Jesus as *political partisans* of a king. In time, to be called Christian would mark a man or woman as anti-Roman, not anti-religious. Christians were viewed as threats to the state not because of what they *believed*. Christians were viewed as threats to the state because of who they chose to *obey*.

Rome had little interest in which god or gods people chose to worship. Their concern was political. Imperial. People were allowed their many gods.

But only one king.

Rome's mandate was unambiguous:

Worship your Christ.
Obey Caesar.

Separating sacred from secular was not an issue for idol-worshiping pagans. But for Christians, it was a nonstarter. Jesus was a king who required his subjects to obey him rather than worship him. In the book of Acts, *Christian* is found exclusively on the lips of critics.[2] It was a slur, an insult.

Imagine that.

In the first century, no one asked Christians if they were Christian.

They were *accused* of it.

It was *evident*.

It was evident because of how they *behaved*. Their behavior underscored fidelity to a king.

NOT SO EVIDENT

In 2020 what has been true for some time became evident. We have reduced our faith to faith. Believing is enough. Which leaves us free to pack up our static beliefs, our internalized religion, and run to our political corners of choice. As a result, many, perhaps most, Christians feel more comfortable with and feel they have more in common with people who share their political views than people who share their Christian faith. This is almost always the case when Christianity is reduced to *faith*. But a Christian faith reduced to belief is a faith neither Jesus nor the apostle Paul would have recognized.

When Christianity is reduced to belief, we lose our voice. We lose our distinction. We're easily reduced to a constituency, a voting bloc that can be wined, dined, lied to, and bribed. By reducing Christianity to a pagan bifurcation of sacred and secular, we've abandoned our opportunity—our responsibility—to serve as the conscience of the nation. Once the church relegated Jesus to the role of *forgiver of our sins* rather than *King of our lives*, we opened the door to lesser kings. Thrones never remain empty long.

Consequently, unlike the original Christians, *nobody is accusing us of being members of the party of Christ.*

No politician anywhere is frustrated with the stubborn

Christians in their district who refuse to align themselves publicly with their party and insist instead on behaving like their Lord. Refusing to submit our lives to the Jesus of the Gospels sets us up to be seduced to believe that by leveraging, perfecting, and baptizing the tools and tactics used by the kingdoms of this world, we can further the cause of Christ. Boycotts, voter guides, protests, suing state and local governments, calling out politicians by name from the pulpit—these are the new spiritual disciplines. And if implemented consistently, with God's help, we can take our country back! We can win!

Which would be fantastic if the win really was winning. But Jesus didn't come to win the way we define *win*.

He came to lose. And he invited us to follow him.

We're not in it to win it. We're here for something else. Something the apostle Paul understood the moment he regained his sight. Something Jesus followers in Antioch understood and embraced. Something that changed the world. Something that could change the world again.

WINNING AT WINNING

The apostle Paul defined his win. In doing so, he defined ours as well.

> Though I am free and belong to no one, I have made
> myself a slave to *everyone*, to *win* as many as
> possible.[3]

A slave to *everyone*? Really, Paul? Even members of the other political party? A slave to people you disagree with? Seriously?

It's important to remember that Paul wasn't asking gentiles to recognize the next step in God's unfolding story of redemption. He was asking them to abandon their entire worldview! He wasn't asking folks to add another idol to the mantle. Following Jesus would require them to empty the mantle and destroy their images. Including . . . including household deities linked to the centuries-old tradition of ancestor worship. "Sorry, Granddad. I'm a Christian now. Into the fire you go!"

He continues:

> To the Jews I became like a Jew, to win the Jews. To those under the law I became like one under the law (though I myself am not under the law), so as to win those under the law. To those not having the law I became like one not having the law (though I am not free from God's law but am under Christ's law), so as to win those not having the law.[4]

What a coward.
Poser.
Pretender.

Come on, Paul. Choose a position! You can't stand in the middle. You're either hot or you're cold. Are you afraid of losing followers? Are you trying to have it both ways?

Those were sentiments communicated by a good many conservative church folks toward their pastors in the months leading up to the last election. Pastors, like me, who refused to politicize our churches despite intense pressure and criticism. Our refusal to take a *side* was interpreted as refusal to take a *stand*—though, in fact, we *had* taken a stand. We were correctly and courageously refusing to politicize the *ekklesia* of Jesus. We were demonstrating our commitment to the Great Commission. We refused to alienate half our community by siding with one political party over the other. We chose to stand with Jesus in the messy middle, where problems are solved, rather than capitulate to divisive, broad-brush political talking points.

It's difficult to take a Christlike stand when pressured to choose a political side. It's hard to follow Paul's example when so many in the church prefer we simply preach like pundits. Still, like the apostle Paul, many courageous, gospel-centered pastors weren't in it to win an election. They were in it to win *people*. They weren't in it to save America.

They were in it to save Americans.

Americans on both sides as well as those on no side of the political divide. They were accused of being fearful when, in fact, they were remaining faithful, despite pressure from deacons, elders, and donors to do otherwise.

I faced—and continue to face—my share of criticism.

Dozens of families reached out to let me know they were leaving our churches because I had bought into the Democratic narrative. When was I going to take a stand? What was I afraid of?

It was disappointing. Discouraging. But no one threatened to feed me to wild animals or substitute me for a tiki torch.

For the record, Paul's stubborn refusal to take a side *then* is why his letters are available to us and are relevant for us *now*. His willingness to stand alone against unimaginable pressure to do otherwise is why his letters and his story shaped Western civilization. What he writes next is one of my favorite statements in the New Testament. It's his mission and strategy statement. First his strategy:

I have become all things to all people . . .[5]

Translated: I'm a spy! I do whatever is necessary to blend in with my surroundings. I work hard not to blow my cover. I've learned to build and navigate relationships with people I have virtually nothing in common with.

But why? Sounds like a lot of work.

. . . so that by all possible means . . .[6]

All possible means. Gotta love that. Whatever it takes. Including being misunderstood and mistreated. Then he lays out his mission. His Great Commission–informed mission:

. . . so that by all possible means I might *save* some.[7]

Paul was forced to navigate the narrow space between three opposing worldviews: (1) first-century Judaism, (2) an empire that assumed its power was by divine design, and (3) local pagan deities scattered throughout the empire— each of which had long histories that galvanized a worldview fueled mostly by superstition and fear.

He had his work cut out for him. There were three buckets, and he didn't fit in any of them.

It's amazing anything Paul did or wrote survived his lifetime. But it did. It did in part because he refused to subjugate his calling and convictions to the prevailing worldviews and power structures. Paul believed YHWH had done something new in the world, for the world, in spite of everything going on around the world. And he was convinced he held the moral and ethical high ground despite being virtually alone in that conviction. He didn't feel compelled to win. Because of what Jesus had done, he'd already won. The world had won. Someone just needed to tell 'em. So Paul set out to do just that.

Paul didn't align himself with the temple, the empire, or with any local priesthood. His willingness to stand apart, to stand alone, positioned him to become the most effective advocate of our faith who has ever lived.

FINDING COMMON GROUND

Paul was brilliant and instructive in his ability to find and leverage common ground with both Jews and pagans. But he never—as in never, ever—leveraged the gospel or the teaching of Jesus to further their agendas. His was a message for people on both sides of all aisles.

To the pagans in Athens, he declared:

> In the *past* God overlooked such ignorance, but *now* he commands all people everywhere to repent.[8]

God had been patient with their pagan ways. They hadn't known any better. But that was then. This is now. Something new had transpired. Someone new had come. And he had come for the benefit of all people.

To Jews and gentiles in Galatia, he wrote:

> There is neither Jew nor Gentile, neither slave nor free, nor is there male and female, for you are all one in Christ Jesus.[9]

This statement was more scandalous than we have time to unpack here. But the point remains: Paul called people *out*.

He did not align himself *with*.

He called people out of their old identities, away from embedded cultural categories. He invited people to leave something behind and adopt something new. Brand stand-alone new. Something so different, so new, it could not be blended with, subjugated to, or co-opted by any agenda other than the intended agenda of its founder. Maintaining his rather lonely position outside any of the prevailing worldviews enabled Paul to build common ground and launch communities of faith. And what fueled his laser-focused mission? He tells us:

> I have become all things to all people so that by all possible means I might save some. I do all this for the sake of the *gospel*, that I may share in its blessings.[10]

Let's do that.
Again.

SAVING AMERICA

When a local church becomes preoccupied with saving *America* at the expense of saving *Americans*, it has forsaken its mission. When church leaders embrace and grow comfortable with save-*America* rhetoric that alienates some *Americans*, they are derelict in their duty. When pastors and churches intentionally or unintentionally subjugate winning people to winning elections, they've already lost.

Even if they win.

The excitement and enthusiasm politically active and aligned congregations experience is not the spirit of God. It's not the spirit of God because they are no longer in sync with the mission of God. Jesus was clear on this point when he commissioned his first-century followers. He charged his earliest followers with a monumental task that came prepackaged with monumental promise. He concluded his Great Commission with a *conditional* promise that we've gotten in the habit of quoting as if it has no conditions.

> Surely I am with *you* always, to the very end of the age.[11]

Who is the *you* included in the *I am with you*?

This *you* extended beyond the folks in his immediate audience. After all, Jesus suggests there would be *yous* making disciples to the very end of the age. So who is *you*? Whom did Jesus promise to be *with*, work *through*, contend *for*?

This promise is promised exclusively to those who prioritize his priority.

Believers whose primary ambition is to make disciples of all nations. Believers who are willing to navigate and maintain relationships with all kinds of people in order to "save some" and "win some."[12] Jesus followers who embrace a "by all possible means" mindset.

The church or church leader who publicly aligns with a political party has relinquished their ability to make disciples of half their own nation, much less all nations. Intentionally—or even unintentionally—aligning a local church with a party or candidate is an insurmountable obstacle to making disciples of those in the other party. Doing so alienates half the population.

The church or church leader who aligns with a political party is disqualified from Jesus's "you." If that describes you, that should concern you. It certainly concerns me.

So, one more time.

With feeling.

Saving *America* is not the mission of the church.

The moment our love or concern for country takes precedence over our love for the people in our country, we are off mission. When saving America diverts energy, focus, and reputation away from saving Americans, we no longer qualify as the *ekklesia* of Jesus. We're merely political tools. A manipulated voting demographic. A photo op. Again, we lose our elevated position as the conscience of the nation. We give up the moral and ethical high ground. As Tim Keller writes,

> "When the church as a whole is no longer seen as speaking to questions that transcend politics, and when it is no longer united by a common faith that transcends politics, then the world sees strong evidence that Nietzsche, Freud, and Marx were right, that religion is really just a cover for people wanting to get their way in the world."[13]

In the months leading up to the 2020 election, politicized congregations and church leaders overplayed their hands. It was painfully obvious they wanted to "get their way in the world." Yes, they had Bible verses to support their desire to "get their way in the world." But one thing they did not have was the support of their Savior.

Now, in case you're wondering, yes, I love my country. Deeply. But when I die, I won't go to Washington, DC. Neither will you. And neither will your neighbors or their kids. The issue is not patriotism. The issue is priority. As a reminder, every time you place your hand over your heart and recite the Pledge of Allegiance, you declare the priority I'm advocating for:

"One Nation under God"

God first.
Nation second.
Our ultimate allegiance is to a King who came to reverse the order of things—the King who rather than requiring his subjects to die for him, died for them instead.

That's a better King.

And our uncompromising devotion to our better King will ultimately make America a better nation.

THEY DON'T MIX

I didn't want to, nor did I have time to, write this book. But my heart is broken over the division—not in our nation but in the church.

Division.

Division is the very thing Jesus was most concerned

about[14]—the thing we seem completely *un*concerned about. Truth is, we've fostered and fueled division by allowing recent political and cultural mayhem to distract us from what our Savior commanded us to do. Consequently, our primary concerns often mirror the concerns of our political party of choice rather than our Savior of choice. And what concerns your political party most? The same thing the other party is most concerned about: winning.

When winning replaces following, we're able to sanctify all manner of un-Jesus-like means to justify that end. We become quick to speak and slow to think. We criticize unbelievers for behaving like unbelievers. We criticize other believers without talking to them first. We rebrand slander as truth-telling. We claim, defend, and sue to ensure that our rights take priority over defending the rights of others. We believe the worst. We rejoice when our enemies stumble. Saving America takes precedence over loving the American next door. And, given enough time, we can produce chapter and verse to support all of it. Actually, given enough time, you can produce chapter and verse to support just about anything.

Perhaps that's why Jesus invited us to follow *him* rather than our *interpretation* of a sacred text. Follow Jesus through the Gospels and you'll find no justification for any of the above.

When winning replaces following, we are no longer following. We are no longer Christian as defined by the folks who originally coined the term.

THE MIX

We've been told not to mix politics and religion. If by *religion* we're referring to private prayers to and corporate worship of a God who is concerned primarily with private prayers and corporate worship, then, yeah. Don't mix 'em. Actually, you can't mix 'em. They exist in two entirely different realms. One in the real world. One in somebody's imagination.

But if by *religion* we're talking about God becoming flesh and making his dwelling among us and instructing us how to behave? If we're talking about God taking on human flesh so we could understand who he is, what he likes, who he likes, and how we should treat the folks he likes? That's a whole other thing.

That's the invasion of one realm by the other.

That's good news.

That's the kingdom of God come near.[15] That's the kingdom of God come to town.

That's what first-century Jesus followers in Antioch were convinced had happened. And as we will discover, once they were convinced, they did not switch *religions*.

They switched *loyalties*.

They switched *kings*.

And it was evident.

Let's make our allegiance to Jesus *evident* again.

CHAPTER TWO

CULTURE WAR CHRISTIANITY ◄

Most Americans recognize that everything is unnecessarily politicized and polarized. And other than the folks who profit from it, nobody likes it. Nobody likes it because, for the most part, Americans agree on the fundamentals. A September 2020 study by Harvard's Carr Center for Human Rights shows that eight in ten Americans believe that "without our freedoms America is nothing."[1] Of those studied, 93 percent say the right to privacy is important, and 92 percent agree that the right to a quality education matters and that racial equality matters. Seven in ten Americans believe they have more in common with one another than not.[2]

So what's the problem?

What's fueling the tension and division?

In a word: fear.

Fear is the fuel.

The sad truth is, the fear fueling our division has been created, cultivated, and stoked by those who benefit from it. Fear is profitable. Media companies want engagement and fear drives engagement. Wannabe leaders need followers. Fear draws followers. Fear-based messaging is nearly twice as effective as messaging that fails to stir that emotion.[3]

Fear is motivating. It motivates us to shut our minds, hearts, and hands. It makes us smaller. More insecure. As Cherie Harder put it, "Dwelling on fear and outrage is spiritually deforming."[4] It's spiritually deforming because fear entices us to place our faith in the person, party, or platform that promises to protect us from whatever they've convinced us we should fear.

For decades, politicians have played to our deepest fears. The other party, the other candidate, is out to destroy everything we value. The other party doesn't care about your family or your values. They don't care about America. And for a donation of twenty-five, fifty, or one hundred dollars, they will protect you, your family, and our great nation.

Nothing divides like politics because nothing divides like fear.

But it's not just politicians.

Pastors and prominent Christian leaders have done their share of fear-mongering as well. They've stoked the imaginations and capitalized on the concerns of their congregants, followers, and mailing list subscribers. They've contributed to the image of the godless Democrats and the soulless Republicans. Kristin Du Mez sums it up disturbingly well: "Evangelical militancy is often depicted as a response to fear. . . . But it's important to recognize that in many cases evangelical leaders actively stoked fear in the hearts of their followers in order to consolidate their own power and advance their own interests."[5]

There are three primary psychological responses to fear: fight, flight, or freeze.[6] There's little money to be raised or influence to be gained with options two and three. But option one? Fight? That's always a win for those looking to win. After all, what's the outcome of a fight? A winner. And so we find ourselves embroiled in yet another round of culture wars.

Leading up to the 2020 election, it wasn't difficult for religious leaders to turn the faithful into culture warriors. With emotions already frayed and fear as the predominant emotion, the fields were ripe for harvest. Add to that the unremitting stream of attack ads clogging our mailboxes and saturating the airways and it took very little effort for church leaders and faith leaders to mobilize their congregants and constituents.

All in Jesus's name, of course.

For pastors and churches comfortable identifying with the Republican or Democratic Party, the 2020 election cycle was a dream come true. For the rest of us, not so much.

November's contest gave both sides the opportunity to take the culture war to new intoxicating and toxic levels. The demonization of everyone in the other party was fair game. We heard it from pundits and pastors alike. It was applauded and amened. I listened in horror as a Baptist pastor I've known for years made light of then-candidate Joe Biden's memory during a sermon introduction—a sermon on renewing the mind. In my home state of Georgia, Republicans were caricatured as heartless racists who wanted to make it illegal to provide water to folks waiting in line to vote. The examples are endless. We all witnessed it. And what we witnessed destroyed our witness. There's no gentle way to say it. Pastors who publicly aligned themselves and their churches with a political party or candidate abandoned their calling, undermined their credibility, and exploited the body of Christ. For them, the end would justify the means. Winning would be worth it. The winner would have the opportunity to determine the direction of our nation for decades to come. So battle lines were drawn. Jesus's name was invoked. And in the end, nobody really won. We still can't agree on who won. The only clear outcome is that the church lost.

The problem with the culture war is that there aren't just winners and losers. There are casualties. When the church takes a leading role in the fray, the casualty is always the faith of the next generation. Their faith is sacrificed on the altar of temporary power and political gain.

"THIS FEELS LIKE WAR"

Culture wars are nothing new, of course, especially when we consider the relatively short history of our nation. University of Virginia sociologist James Davison Hunter coined the phrase *culture wars* in 1991. He explained the origin of the phrase in an interview with the *Wall Street Journal*: "As I was interviewing people back in the '80s and then into the '90s, the activists who were involved in it all said—left and right—this feels like war."[7]

In his landmark book, *Culture Wars: The Struggle to Define America*, Hunter argues that while Americans hold a wide range of moral commitments and political priorities, they are often portrayed as holding one of two distinct worldviews competing in an epic, unresolvable struggle.

In a culture war, a dispute takes place "between groups who hold fundamentally different views of the world," writes Hunter. "On all sides the contenders are generally sincere, thoughtful, and well-meaning, but they operate with fundamentally opposing visions of the meaning of America: what it has been, what it is, and what it should be."[8]

In the 1990s, those on the front lines of the culture wars were evangelical pastors and leaders, many of whom pushed the idea that faithfully following Jesus meant the church must take control of major spheres of influence in society, even if that required aligning with political movements to gain power. Their language was often militaristic. They spoke of "invading enemy territory," "occupying hostile institutions," and "taking over secular society" to create "godly change" in America. Instead of viewing culture through the lens of compassionate and winsome engagement, these church leaders saw it as a system to be conquered.

I had a front row seat to this effort.

It's why I'm convinced that not only does this approach

not work, it is antithetical to the mission of the church, Jesus's new-covenant command, and common sense.

As author and commentator David French notes, the culture war approach "often confuses Christian power with biblical justice, and it creates incentives for Christians to not just seek power but to feel a sense of failure and emergency when they are not in positions of cultural or political control."[9]

What he says next is worth pausing to catch your breath: "Any admonition that declares that we must rule should be checked with the immediate reminder that Christ did not. It is the cross—not the boardroom, not the Oval Office, and not the box office—that is the absolute center of the Kingdom of God."[10]

Yes, it is.

Jesus did not come to win as we define winning. That's why we're still talking about him, and most Americans couldn't name their senators if their lives depended on it.

A FUTILE FIGHT!

Fallout from our cultural disputes and quests for power has ranged from minor skirmishes and sound bites to national demonstrations, boycotts, and violent protests. Today, of course, it also includes social media outrage. But the dirty little secret of culture war advocates, both religious and nonreligious, is that they cannot afford to claim victory, or they lose followers and funding. So both sides claim to be *losing*. That's how they *win*. The entire endeavor is fueled by fear. Both sides of any culture war conflict need an enemy to survive. They need an enemy to exist. This is why Christians and the church in particular should refuse to participate. There is no win because the goal isn't winning—the goal is warring. You *can't* love your enemy in that scenario because you aren't supposed to love your enemy. Conflict *is* the win. There is no middle ground, and there is no room for compromise. This is one of several reasons Jesus refused to take sides in the culture wars of his era.

Washington, DC–based theologian and political theorist Jonathan Leeman contends that when it comes to culture, Jesus followers must neither withdraw nor seek to control, but rather faithfully represent the values of the King we serve. He says,

> A losing team becomes desperate and takes desperate measures. But what might it look like for the church's politics if we became convinced—really convinced—both that we will have trouble in this world and that Jesus has overcome this world, as he promised? Might we present a strange and winsome confidence that is not desperate to win the culture wars but is also tenderly and courageously committed to the good of others? . . .
>
> Anyone who tells you, "Withdraw, we're losing!" or, "Push forward, we're winning!" may have

succumbed to a kind of utopianism, as if we could build heaven on earth. Instead, heaven starts in our assemblies, even if only as in a mirror dimly. Christians are heaven's ambassadors, and our churches are its embassies. Neither panic nor triumphalism becomes us. A cheerful confidence does. We represent this heavenly and future kingdom now, whether the skies are cloudy or clear.[11]

A BETTER ENDEAVOR

There are certainly things worth fighting for. But not as many as we might imagine. Beware the leader who scares you to recruit you to fight for a cause that was previously unknown to you, especially if the recruiter stands to gain from your efforts.

Jesus's refusal to take sides in the culture wars of his day was not because he lacked opinions or conviction. He wasn't afraid to take a stand. Jesus knew what we can't seem to get our heads around: that when the church chooses a side, as defined by any political party, we've sided against people on the other side. In that moment, we elevate our potentially flawed views over people. For Jesus, a *you* always took precedence over a *view*. This drove his friends and adversaries nuts. At times it made him look inconsistent. But he was calculatingly consistent. His purpose precluded him from joining forces with either side of any cultural issue. His refusal to take sides was not out of a lack of concern.

It was because what concerned him most precluded him from doing so.

As I will remind you throughout this book, Jesus was a king who came to reverse the order of things. He gave his life for his subjects rather than requiring them to lay down their lives for him. In political and imperial terms, Jesus lost. After his resurrection, he invited his closest friends to choose to lose as well and to dedicate their lives to convincing as many people as they could to join his losers' club. His words:

"Make disciples of all nations."[12]

A disciple is a follower. Jesus followers in Antioch were following so well that they were accused of being little Christs. Christians. When Jesus gave what we appropriately refer to as his Great Commission, he did not leave the content of their disciple-making venture up to them. He said (and you can probably quote this by heart),

". . . teaching them to obey everything I have commanded you."[13]

Jesus's most recent *command* at that point was "Love each other as I have loved you,"[14] followed by, "You are my friends if you do what I command."[15]

This may come as a shock.

You can't make disciples of people you demonize publicly

and label as enemies of the faith or the state. As Ed Stetzer asserts, "You can't hate people and engage them with the gospel at the same time. You can't war with people and show the love of Jesus. You can't be both outraged and on mission."[16]

Jesus didn't come to help any particular group succeed with *their thing*. He came to establish his own thing. His assembly. His *ekklesia*. His kingdom—a kingdom not of this world but very much for this world. A kingdom fueled by an others-first ethic that stood in sharp contrast to the winner-take-all, win-at-all-costs ethic that fuels the kingdoms of this world.

The moment we step into a ring that requires someone to lose in order for us to win, we are no longer followers of Jesus. I saw this play out in the 1980s and again in the '90s. Different issues, same approach, same outcome—loss of influence with culture and loss of respect by the next generation.

Politically active pastors and churches, by nature of their public affiliation, eliminate common ground with anyone associated with or sympathetic to the other party. It's politics first, faith second . . . or perhaps third. It's *One God under Nation* . . . There's no getting around it. Politically associated churches attempt to leverage Jesus for an agenda other than the agenda of Jesus.

Judas tried that.

Leveraging Jesus, the teaching of Jesus, or the *ekklesia* of Jesus for a purpose other than the mission of Jesus is just another way to gain the whole world and lose our souls. And our influence.

Peter and Paul were executed for refusing to prioritize the state over their faith. Christians in the first, second, and third centuries were arrested, beheaded, fed to wild animals, and burned alive because they refused to prioritize allegiance to the state over allegiance to the commands of Christ.

Let that sink in.

Heroes of the faith, men who penned the Scripture, men and women responsible for collecting and protecting the documents of our faith—they were often violently executed for refusing to do the very thing politically aligned pastors and church leaders have done unapologetically in their churches, on national television, and on social media.

Publicly aligning a local church behind a political party or candidate is betrayal, pure and simple. Jesus didn't come to upgrade or fix something. He came to rule in our hearts and reign over our behavior. He claimed the role of master and commander-in-chief of those who would acknowledge his right to rule. He was not and is not a religious figure. He is a king.

No one can serve two religions.

Said nobody.

"No one can serve two masters."[17]

Said our Master.

> "Either you will hate the one and love the other,
> or you will be devoted to the one and *despise* the
> other."[18]

For far too long, far too many of us have *despised* the Master by editing and reimagining him so as to recruit him to our political party of choice. But follow Jesus through the Gospels and you'll discover he cannot be recruited. He does not take sides. And if the authors of the New Testament are correct, one day he will take over.

When Christianity is reduced to *belief*, we leave the door open for someone else to *rule*. When Christianity is reduced to belief, it's easy to decorate our politics with the symbols, sayings, and relics of the Christian faith. Christianity reduced to sacred, religious belief is a version of Christianity that first-century Jesus followers would not have recognized.

Our faith is not an ornament. It's not an adjective. There are no Christian Republicans. There are no Christian Democrats. You can't have two masters. Having two masters didn't work in the first century. And it doesn't work now. Until we let go of our infatuation with winning, we will continue to be divided. We will continue responding to culture and change as if we have no choice but to play by the rules of the kingdoms of this world. Consequently, we will continue to be used, leveraged, and, ultimately, ignored.

By the way, we should fear being ignored more than we fear being persecuted. Jesus followers have a celebrated history of one but not the other.

Public alignment with a candidate or party is a betrayal of the church's *imperative*, our mandate, to make disciples. Anything that serves as an obstacle to that simple imperative should be eliminated from a local church. Whatever or whoever distracts us from our Lord's final instructions should be set aside. As James, the brother of Jesus, famously said,

> It is my judgment, therefore, that *we should not make it difficult* for the Gentiles who are turning to God.[19]

What about Republicans who are turning or returning to God? What about Democrats who are turning or returning to God?

When pastors and Christian leaders publicly participate in culture wars, we make it hard for those who are turning to God to find God. With each inflammatory political post on social media, we make Jesus secondary and politics primary. Disparaging words about anyone who voted for "that candidate" push people away from our Jesus.

SCARING THE KIDS

As I mentioned earlier, the next generation is usually a casualty when the church steps into the culture war arena.

Many have noted how millennials and Gen Z are convinced that evangelicals are double-stitch sewn into the hip pocket of the Republican Party. Russell Moore summarizes what pastors all over the country have observed: "We now see young evangelicals walking away from evangelicalism not because they do not believe what the church teaches, but because they believe the *church itself* does not believe what the church teaches."[20]

Moore goes on to point out that this generation isn't leaving the church because they disapprove of Jesus. They are leaving because they're convinced that the church itself disapproves of Jesus! And they aren't alone.

The Public Religion Research Institute reported in 2016 that of the Americans who've left their childhood religion in adulthood, 16 percent said they did so because their church was too focused on politics.[21] Hundreds of thousands of people are represented in that statistic.

They didn't leave the church because they found Jesus less compelling. They left because the church didn't find Jesus compelling enough. They recognized that when a church or church leader publicly lines up behind a candidate or party, they have abandoned the mission of Jesus.

Here's a question I ask church leaders every chance I get:

What is the faith of the next generation worth?

Before they can answer, I answer for them:

Everything!

Not so sure? Let me rephrase the question:

What is the faith of your children worth?

Everything?
You sure?
What is the faith of your grandchildren worth? What is
the faith of your niece or nephew worth? At the beginning
of this past election cycle, I asked the folks in our churches
the following question:

Are you more concerned about your kid's political
views or their faith?

We all know the correct answer. But instead of immediately answering, pay attention to the tension that question
creates in you. You'll discover something. You may discover
that your politics are contending for lordship. Perhaps your
political party of choice has become your primary identity
marker rather than your faith. Perhaps you're guilty of *one
God under Nation*.

That's difficult to admit. It's difficult to admit because
it's difficult to recognize. It's difficult to recognize because
we've become good at proof-texting our political views.
We're more than willing to allow our pastor, author, or

leader of choice to proof-text our views for us. Mix in a double dose of confirmation bias and desirability bias, and we have a cocktail that blinds us to *whose* we truly are.

But it doesn't have to be this way.

It hasn't always been this way.

There is another way. Once upon a time it was called *The Way*.

CHAPTER THREE

CANCELED

In July 2020—during the height of the COVID-19 crisis—CNN invited me to explain the thinking behind our decision to suspend in-person services at our Atlanta-area churches for the remainder of the year. I told my host that our decision to suspend in-person gatherings was our way of loving our neighbors and protecting our neighborhoods as Jesus commanded us to do. I went on to explain that our churches are not closed.[1]

I went on to talk about the innovative ways we were serving the underserved people most affected by the pandemic. I was glad CNN contacted me rather than Fox News. The CNN audience trends more progressive and less religious than FNN.

I bet you knew that.

The point being, I was excited to have an opportunity to talk about Jesus on a network that doesn't often feature positive stories about evangelical churches or evangelical faith leaders.

So imagine my surprise when the following afternoon a

friend and longtime church attendee called to let me know how disappointed he was that I was "on CNN." When I asked why, he insisted it undermined my credibility. And he was particularly offended that I said, "The church is not an essential service."

Which I did say.

But I said it within the context of a specific question asked by my host. I was referencing the necessity or essentialness of meeting indoors, shoulder to shoulder during a pandemic. I was not referencing the importance or essentialness of the church in general.

The longer my friend talked, the more apparent it became that he had not seen the interview. So I asked him, straight up, "Did you watch the interview?"

"No, I don't watch CNN. Somebody sent me an article about what you said."

I was shocked. He hadn't taken the time to track down and watch the interview before calling to chastise me for doing it. He drew a conclusion about his friend and pastor based on an article written by someone he's never met, posted on a right-leaning "Christian" website that rarely has anything good to say about me or our churches.

It was disturbing. It was par for the election-season course.

He was more upset about *where* I said what I said than *what* I said. He didn't even know what I had actually said. Why not instead:

Wow, Andy, I'm so glad that secular, anti-Christian, fake-news organization interviewed our pastor and gave him an opportunity to talk about what our church is doing in the community in Jesus's name.

That would have required interpreting my appearance on CNN within the context of everything he knew about me from years of life together. But that's not how it's done these days. These days, past performance and context are irrelevant—unless past performance and context fit a preferred narrative. Apparently, believing the best is a relic of a bygone era as well.

One of the many things I appreciate about Jesus is that he was never concerned about guilt by association. If he had been, he would have stayed in heaven. He would have certainly refused to associate with me.

And perhaps you.

SOMETHING OLD, SOMETHING NEW

Cancel culture isn't new. Just the name is. People have been canceling other people since the days of Cain and Abel. The Pharisees canceled Jesus. The Judaizers canceled Paul. Once Emperor Constantine lifted the ban on Christian worship, it took the church about twenty minutes to start canceling their own to garner imperial favor and power. Being canceled by the church was particularly painful leading up to and throughout the Reformation.

I was raised Southern Baptist. We canceled pretty much everybody except other Southern Baptists. If I'm remembering correctly, nobody suggested canceling adulterous King David or his even more adulterous, idol-worshiping son, Solomon.

Just wanted to make sure you were paying attention.

I doubt you need a definition for *cancel culture*. But just in case you do, here's a thoughtful description from our friends at Dictionary.com.

1. The phenomenon or practice of publicly rejecting, boycotting, or ending support for particular people or groups because of their socially or morally unacceptable views or actions. . . .
2. The shared attitudes and values within a particular segment of society that lead to such public rejection of particular people or groups. *In a cancel culture, we appoint ourselves the arbiters of right and wrong.*[2]

Sounds harmless when reduced to a definition. But the reality is anything but.

The reality is that if you say one thing I disagree with or don't like, I discount *everything* you've ever said, along with everything you've ever accomplished.

You're dead to me.

Beyond the personal harm inflicted by this insidious and insane trend, there are broader consequences:

Cancel culture lowers the IQ of the entire culture.

It lowers our IQ because we are no longer willing to listen to or learn from individuals or groups who don't see, interpret, and experience the world the way we do. Canceling an individual or group produces nothing while undermining a fundamental catalyst for progress, namely, the unfiltered exchange of ideas, opinions, and *insight* without the necessity of anyone always *being right.*

Cancel culture cancels the right to be wrong.

It cancels the right to be partially wrong but still heard. It cancels our willingness to appreciate and learn from the highlight reels of those we disagree with or who later say something offensive, bigoted, or racist. The implication being, we should remain open to learning only from those who are as perfect as we are—as we define perfect.

Dr. Jill McCorkel, a professor of sociology and criminology at Villanova University, views cancel culture as the modern version of banishment.[3] She's right. Individuals, brands, bands, shows, movies, authors, networks—nobody is safe. People are losing jobs—and, in some cases, careers—because of things they said or did in high school. Not illegal things. Adolescent things. Imagine a sixteen-year-old acting like a sixteen-year-old.

The nerve.

It's gotten so bad that in July 2020, *Harper's Magazine* published an open letter denouncing cancel culture and calling for an end to what the editors viewed as an excuse for intolerance, public shaming, and censorship. Over 150 public figures signed the letter, including J. K. Rowling, Malcolm Gladwell, Cornel West, and Fareed Zakaria, just to name four. Not surprisingly, thousands took to Twitter to cancel the cancelation. And while they were at it, they canceled many of the signers as well.

The moment we become so myopic as to allow a single moment to cancel the work and accomplishments of a lifetime, we have embraced a standard to which we hope never to be held accountable ourselves. Which makes us hypocrites. We expect grace and forgiveness for our indiscretions while having predecided not to extend the same to others.

Then there's this.

Whose voice, influence, and opinion did you attempt to cancel when you were thirteen? Most likely the voice, influence, and opinion of the people who birthed, fed, and housed you. Then you got older. Over time you learned to appreciate the opinion and perspective of your imperfect providers. The point being, as difficult as it is to admit, *sometimes we're wrong.*

Sometimes folks we don't particularly like and don't want to be like get it right. Sometimes Democrats are right. Sometimes Republicans are right. Sometimes the other side is partially right. But if we close ourselves off to everything they say, we miss the part we're missing . . . which means we're missing something.

CANCEL ME

From time to time, I've found myself on the receiving end of cancel culture—almost always by other Christians. It's fascinating. I save my juiciest cancel Tweets to share with the kids over dinner. Here's a sampling:

> @AndyStanley You are a heretic! Repent, before it's too late. You are a cancer to the body of Christ.

> @AndyStanley you are a false teacher. Telling people not to believe the Bible. The Lord has a nice warm place waiting for you on judgment day.

Following an interview with _Outreach_ magazine:

> @AndyStanley you can sit down with all the lukewarm effeminate magazines you want, brother. Know this, the Lord reads the heart and you WILL stand before him. You are to publicly repent of your heretical teaching. I forgive you but you need to renounce your heresies.

> @AndyStanley ought to go silent and finish his days in repentant mourning.

And last but not least:

@AndyStanley You have got to be with Satan.

Perhaps.

Sandra and I are always fascinated by the Twitter bios of my critics. They include descriptions such as:

Jesus lover.
Proud parent of . . .
Saved by the grace of God.
Jesus is my King!

Reconciling their self-portrayals with their vitriolic rhetoric is difficult. But obviously they don't see a problem with it.

On the rare occasion that one of my social media critics actually follows me on Twitter, I always try to engage them in conversation. Always. The temperature immediately drops. They assumed I would never see their comments, much less respond—and much, much less share them with my kids at dinner. They usually begin by telling me how much they love my dad. Then I send 'em free books. As many as they want. After all, I'm a Christian.

Christians are reconciled people who've been given the ministry of reconciliation.

Reconciling is more productive than canceling, right?
Jesus thought so.

Navigating social media criticism and friending my critics has become a hobby of sorts. But in 2020 the canceling and criticism hit much closer to home.

In 2020 I found myself on the receiving end of cancel culture from church members. Dozens of 'em. Emails. Voicemails. DMs. Letters. Couples showing up at the office. Most of these folks were longtime church attendees who wrote or showed up to let me know they were leaving the church because of our decision to suspend in-person weekend worship services.

During a pandemic.

Call me crazy.

I was reminded on more than one occasion that a *more famous than me* high-profile pastor, who was not afraid to take a stand, announced to his congregation, "There is no pandemic." So perhaps there wasn't.

But I thought there was.

More importantly, the folks our churches are attempting to influence thought there was.

As it turned out, our decision to suspend weekend gatherings was not the real reason folks chose to leave our church in 2020. I know that to be the case because I called 'em. I called everybody for whom we could find a phone number. After I convinced them that it was really me calling, the fun began.

In 100 percent of the cases, they began the conversation by telling me how much the church had meant to them and their families. One gentleman gave me a detailed account of how our church saved his marriage. He went on for so long, I almost forgot he was leaving. Then I thought, "If I don't interrupt, perhaps he'll talk himself out of leaving."

Multiple folks gushed about how much their children and teenagers enjoyed and benefited from our student environments. Wives told me ours was the only church they could get their husbands to attend and how grateful they were for how we *did church*.

But . . .

Then it got political.

Once the shock that I had actually called wore off, well-worn partisan talking points informed their dialogue. It was obvious. Honestly, I was a bit embarrassed for some of them. They regurgitated stats and opinions they'd heard via their preferred media outlets as if they'd come up with these ideas all by themselves. I couldn't help but assume that they thought I lived in a cave without access to cable news.

Here's a sampling of their reasons for leaving:

Obviously, I had *bought into the Democratic narrative* regarding the virus and masks.

Because I'd *"bowed my knee" to government pressure instead of God*. (In one case I'd *"bowed my knee to Caesar."*)

Because I *refused to take a stand*. Meaning, of course, their stand.

Because I had become *more concerned about being popular than preaching the truth*.

Because I had *embraced a left-wing, Marxist agenda*.

For these reasons, and others like them, they were out!

In the course of our conversations, I would ask, "What have you heard me say or not say that has led you to this conclusion?" Nobody quoted me. Nobody even pointed to a particular message. It all boiled down to their interpretation of why we suspended live, in-person services. Their *interpretation* overruled my *explanation*. Basically, they didn't believe me. They could not imagine that I decided to suspend in-person worship services just to protect the community. There had to be another reason, an ulterior, politically motivated motive.

The truth is that our decision *was* our way of loving . . . wait for it . . . loving those in our neighborhoods who would have lost respect for us if we had insisted on cramming thousands of adults and children into our buildings despite the health risks, perceived or real. Our decision was intentional and missional.

Folks in our churches who were part of the medical community—Republicans and Democrats—applauded our decision, as did folks who had lost or almost lost loved ones to complications from the virus. A high school senior in our church lost both parents to COVID-19 within four days of each other.

What I didn't hear—even once—from the people I called was, "Andy, we're leaving because we miss attending church!" There were in fact dozens of families that normally attended one of our churches who elected to attend churches in our communities that reopened earlier than we did. But they didn't write two-page emails including links to articles

I needed to read to explain their decision. And most of those folks returned once we reopened our buildings.

As intense as these conversations were, they always ended well. I made sure of that. Besides, I wasn't offended. Just disappointed. I was saddened that Christians would cancel years of ministry partnership not because of our theology and not because of our political stance. We are apolitical. On purpose. They chose to leave because we refused to take a stand politically. More specifically, we refused to take *their* stand politically.

They would never admit it—because they can't see it— but these folks left because we *refused* to be political. We refused to politicize the *ekklesia* of Jesus. We opted for *under* God.

It was disappointing that folks who served and gave faithfully for years allowed political spin doctors and news-readers to separate them from their faith community. Their political filter was screwed on so tight that everything, including the pandemic, was viewed through the lens of party affiliation. Their decision to leave their church was informed by political talking points, not the teaching of the New Testament—talking points created by and delivered by people who had done nothing to improve their marriages and had never invested a minute in the spiritual development of their children.

Actually, it was more than disappointing.

It was baffling.

Baffling because they didn't leave over something I

said or did. They left because I wouldn't say or do what they were convinced I should say or do. And by their own admission, what they wanted me to say and do had nothing to do with the teaching of Jesus. It was based entirely on partisan spin.

So they canceled their church!

For now anyway.

The good news is that the vast majority of our church community stuck around. Most did far more than just stick around. They led groups in their homes. They hosted driveway groups for students. They participated in outdoor baptism services. And they gave.

Big time.

Every fall, we conduct an ambitious giving campaign we call Be Rich. We lifted the name from Paul's letter to Timothy, where he instructs Timothy to instruct rich people "to be rich in good deeds, and to be generous and willing to share."[4] Most years we raise around $5 million, which we immediately pass along to community charities, both faith-based and non-faith-based. Most of the money goes to organizations that focus on underserved children and families, foster care, food insecurity, and job training. About 12 percent of the funds are allocated to international organizations that focus on similar needs. In September 2020 I challenged our churches to be *more* generous than ever to our Be Rich initiative because the need was greater than ever. Keep in mind, we had not hosted in-person worship services for over six months.

The amazing, mission-minded Jesus followers in our Atlanta-area churches gave over $8 million in four weeks. In 2020.

And then we gave it all away.

In Jesus's name.

In 2021 they gave close to $10 million in five weeks. We gave all of that away as well.

I suppose there are good reasons to cancel a church. But the decision to close buildings full of recirculated air during a pandemic is not one of them.

CANCELING JESUS

For thoughtful Americans, the parasitic nature of cancel culture should be reason enough to steer clear of it. Love of—or, if nothing else, concern for—the social climate of our nation should cause us to resist it when we see it and refuse to participate in it.

But for those of us who publicly identify as Jesus followers, there are additional reasons we should reject cancel culture in all its various expressions—reasons core to who we are and what we profess to believe. Yet despite what should be obvious to anyone who has read even small portions of the Gospels, many Christians are energized by canceling individuals and groups. They appear eager to give up influence with people for whom Christ died. People—if the Gospels are accurate—Jesus chose *not* to cancel. People he refused to banish.

During the most recent presidential election cycle, a handful of high-profile Christian leaders platformed a version of Christianity that is anything but. They condoned, celebrated, encouraged, and participated in slander, character assassination, hyperbole, labeling, and vilifying anyone whose politics didn't line up with their views or their candidate.

It was embarrassing.

It hurt all of us.

I know some of these folks. They taught their children to behave better. Their children should have taken their phones away. They betrayed their Savior, and they abused their influence. Even worse, their irresponsible, adolescent behavior empowered their followers and their congregants to follow suit.

They made it abundantly clear what they thought of political leaders and candidates of the other party: *They are an evil, godless bunch who if given the opportunity will destroy everything good and decent in our nation. Including the church!*

For the sake of argument, let's assume they were correct. Let's assume the folks in the other party—as in *all* the folks in the other party—were anti-family, anti-freedom, anti-God, anti-America, anti-religion, and, above all, anti-church.

Is there anything to be learned from the life and teaching of Jesus regarding our posture and response to a threat of that magnitude?

Yes.

Is there anything to be learned from the apostle Paul in that regard?

Yes.

Would it look or sound anything like the venomous, vitriolic, hyperbolic, win-lose, defensive language employed by Christian leaders during the previous election cycle?

No.

Am I judging them?

Yes.

According to Jesus and the apostle Paul, that's my responsibility. What's not my responsibility—or theirs—is to publicly judge and alienate people outside our faith community, people who never subscribed to our worldview to begin with. Paul was crystal clear on this:

> What business is it of mine to judge those *outside* the church?[5]

Implication: It's none of your business.

> Are you not to judge those inside?[6]

Implication: Yes!

But then who's going to judge all the morally corrupt, anti-god, anti-family, anti-church folks . . . in the other party?

Good question.

Not you. Not me.
Paul tells us:

God will judge those outside.[7]

But if we can't judge 'em out loud, how are Christians supposed to respond to people like that? That's another good question, a question worth considering and talking about. But name-calling on national television and in paid-for speeches is not part of the answer. That's the unfortunate responsibility of political pundits, newsreaders, and public office holders.

But pastors?

Christian leaders?

Have we lost our minds?

Before I disappear down this particular rabbit hole, I need to back up and state what most of us know to be true. Stereotyping and demonizing an entire political party is foolish. All statements that begin with "All Republicans . . ." are inaccurate. All statements that begin with "All Democrats . . ." are equally inaccurate.

All Democrats are not morally corrupt, anti-God, anti-family, and anti-church, and all Republicans are not anti-voting-rights, anti-healthcare, and anti-vaccine. Let's not participate in that type of labeling. This kind of rhetoric divides American from American. It divides Christian from Christian as well.

When white Republican church leaders label Democrats

as immoral, anti-God, and anti-all-things-good, they insult and alienate hundreds of thousands of our God-fearing, Jesus-following, church-serving Black and Brown brothers and sisters. The message, intentional or not, is unambiguous.

> Your political views preclude you from feeling welcome in our church. Worship with us at your own risk.

If you attend or pastor a predominantly white church where demonizing the Democratic Party or party leaders by name is commonplace and applauded, you should put a sign in the lobby that reads,

> We are unapologetically pro-Republican.

Why not?

Why make first-timers unnecessarily uncomfortable? Let 'em know before they drop off their kids. Let 'em know before they get seated in the middle of a row. Let 'em know before you take up the offering. And in keeping with my goal of being an equal opportunity offender, if you attend or pastor a predominantly Black or Brown church that is unapologetically political, you should put up a sign as well.

Why not?

Seriously, why not?

"That's ridiculous, Andy" is not a reason.

Why not let people know that, in addition to the gospel,

your church has a political agenda. Let 'em know that if their political views don't line up with the political views of the leadership of the church, they will never feel at home in your church.

Why not?

The reasons you would never post a sign like that in your church lobby are the same reasons you should eliminate all things partisan from your preaching, teaching, and marketing. Politicizing your church and publicly demonizing the other party is *more* offensive and *more* harmful than a sign that tips people off as to what they *may* experience.

Just something to think about.

WHAT DID JESUS DO?

Back to the question I posed a few paragraphs back:

> Is there anything in the life and teaching of Jesus or the life and teaching of the apostle Paul that's instructive as to how Jesus followers should respond to a culture that appears to be increasingly hostile to our values and beliefs?

Again, yes. But before we go there, we need to ask and answer *the* question that will ultimately determine whether we even allow the life and teaching of Jesus to influence our responses to what's happening culturally, nationally, and politically:

Are we willing to prioritize our faith over our politics?

If not, it doesn't matter what Jesus modeled or what the apostle Paul wrote. As long as we lead with our politics, we will find a way to deconstruct and reimagine Jesus to ensure he fits neatly within our political framework. Political parties have been doing that for decades. Both sides quote Jesus when it serves their purposes. But neither side is committed to the purposes of Jesus.

We shouldn't expect them to be.

But what about us?

If you consider yourself a Christian, of course you are willing to prioritize your faith over your politics. Your faith is why you're a Republican! Right?

Unless, of course, you're a Democrat. In that case, your faith is why you're a Democrat.

Apparently there's a disconnect somewhere. Things aren't as cut-and-dried as we imagine them to be. That's why this is an important question. So let me ask it a different way.

Are you willing to follow Jesus regardless of where he leads you politically?

To tease that out a bit, are you willing to embrace the others-first kingdom ethic of Jesus when it requires you to keep your mouth shut and your opinions to yourself so as not to lose influence with outsiders? Are you willing to serve rather than cancel? Love rather than demonize? Pray for rather than publicly criticize?

If not . . . if that's too passive . . . or too progressive . . . then maybe your politics have become your lord. Maybe, like Judas, you are attempting to co-opt Jesus.

That's difficult to admit.

It's difficult to recognize.

In the next several chapters, we are going to let Jesus and the apostle Paul school us on how to respond to those with whom we disagree and how to navigate a culture that is hostile to what we value and believe.

Throughout, we will be reminded that the early church—inspired by the upside-down kingdom ethic of Jesus yet trapped between a hostile empire and a religious system intent on its destruction—survived, thrived, and shaped Western civilization. How this transpired is one of history's great mysteries.

But it should be no mystery to us.

In an ancient culture that worshiped winning, the message of Jesus was considered weak. Offensive. Appalling. Something to be canceled. Violently, if need be. It was a cancer on the empire and a threat to the temple. But Jesus's others-first value system appealed to many. Christians refused to abandon the sick. They adopted abandoned children. They extended compassion and generosity to people and groups who could not or would not return the favor. They deemed women equal to men. Slaves were to be treated as brothers. In the end what was considered appalling became contagious. It swept through the empire. Against all odds, the message and value system of a Nazarene cult inspired by a crucified teacher would circle the globe.

It was irresistible.

Let's do that again.

For that to happen again, something else must happen first. We must release our death grip on winning politically, along with our faith-destabilizing fear of losing.

We must refuse to play by the rules of the kingdoms of this world. We must choose instead the way of Jesus. The way of the cross. In the shadow of the cross, we lose our right to cancel anybody. We are to forgive as we have been forgiven. We are to let our light shine in such a way that people see our good works, hear our good words, and look up—and glorify our Father in heaven.

Inflammatory rhetoric may win us more social media followers, but it damages our influence with those we are called to reach. Pastors and Christian leaders in particular should never give up influence to make a point—especially a political point.

Besides, if the other party is opposing God's plan for our nation and in desperate need of Jesus, what posture should Jesus followers take? What posture should Jesus followers take toward people who are far from God? Here's a clue from a story so familiar I don't even need to tell it.

> While he was still a long way off, his father saw him and was filled with compassion for him; he ran to his son, threw his arms around him and kissed him.[8]

He "kissed him" because he never canceled him.
He wasn't banished.
He was lost.
Meanwhile,

> The older brother became angry and refused to go in. So his father went out and pleaded with him. But he answered his father, "Look! All these years I've been slaving for you and never disobeyed your orders. Yet you never gave me even a young goat so I could celebrate with my friends. But when this son of yours who has squandered your property with prostitutes comes home, you kill the fattened calf for him!"[9]

That's what canceled looks like and sounds like. It's ugly. But I love the next part. We all love the next part.

> "My son," the father said, "you are always with me, and everything I have is yours. But we had to celebrate and be glad, because this brother of yours was dead and is alive again; he was lost and is found."[10]

So what posture should Jesus followers take toward people who are far from God and in need of a Savior?

It was Christianity, not the Democratic or Republican Party, that shaped Western civilization. It was the teaching of Jesus, not the planks of our current political platforms, that laid the foundation for our modern sense of justice, fairness, and dignity. Throughout our very short history as a nation, both of our current parties have gotten it wrong. During our short history as a nation, multiple parties turned out the lights because their party was over. During our short history, political leaders from both parties have fallen short morally and fallen short in their leadership.

So why would followers of the King who did not come to be served but to serve and to give his life for the men and women in the party you dislike, prioritize allegiance to and allow ourselves to be divided by the promises of lesser kings? Why would we allow a political *view* to divide us from a living, breathing *you*? A *you* for whom Christ died? For Jesus followers, a *you* is always more important than a political *view*.

Jesus is not a footnote in a political platform. He did not come to support or refine an existing political system or world order. He came to replace what was in place. He came to cancel sin and to restore men and women of all nations and all political persuasions to himself.

When we reimagine Jesus to fit our partisan agendas, we rob the world of the message that changed the world.

We cancel the message that canceled our sin.

PART
TWO

OUR
HISTORY

CHAPTER FOUR

KINGDOMS IN CONFLICT ◀

Chances are you're familiar with the name Bart Ehrman. Bart is a New Testament scholar and author. He's written and edited over thirty books, six of which earned their way to the *New York Times* bestsellers list. Currently, he serves as a professor of religious studies at the University of North Carolina at Chapel Hill. He has degrees from Moody Bible Institute, Wheaton College, and Princeton Theological Seminary.

And Bart is an atheist.

In 2018, Bart Ehrman published *The Triumph of Christianity: How a Forbidden Religion Swept the World.* In it, Ehrman attempts to unravel one of history's great mysteries, perhaps history's *greatest* mystery—namely, how did a first-century movement launched by a dozen or so Galileans gain traction in the ancient world and go on to become a catalyst for cultural change that shaped the modern world? How did it come about that Rome replaced their entire pantheon of gods with a Galilean rabbi crucified by one of their own governors? A rabbi who claimed to be a king and thus a threat to the empire. No one denies any of this happened. The question is *how*?

It's an important question for us in particular because the answer to that question is the answer to a question evangelical Christians have been wrestling with for decades.

What will it take to bring about revival in America?

Specifically, what will it take to bring about a revival of biblical values, virtues, and ethics of such magnitude that it would alter the culture of our country?

What most Christians and, apparently, most Christian leaders overlook is that the very change they hope to see in our nation in this generation happened on an even grander scale in another nation in a previous generation.

Exhibit A: A cross hangs over the emperor's entrance to the Roman Colosseum.

When the Colosseum was constructed, crosses were ubiquitous throughout the empire. But they didn't adorn buildings. They were adorned with naked men gasping for air and begging for a quick death. The cross was not merely a method of execution. It was an instrument of terror, a perfected blend of suffering and shame. It was a reminder to the world that Caesar was lord and Rome was eternal.

But the cross at the emperor's entrance to the Colosseum doesn't represent Roman crucifixion in general. It represents *one* crucifixion: the crucifixion of Jesus of Nazareth. His crucifixion would be the catalyst for the cessation of crucifixion as a form of punishment.

In the first century, the cross represented the cruelty of an empire. By the fifth century, it represented the love of God. In the eighteenth century, Pope Benedict XIV declared the Roman Colosseum a sacred monument dedicated to the suffering of Christ. Don't rush by that fact.

The Roman Colosseum is now a monument to the suffering of *Jesus*—the same Jesus who was viewed as a threat to the empire and consequently crucified by the empire.

How did that happen? What was the catalyst for cultural change of that magnitude? We should know the answer to that question.

As part of his declaration, Pope Benedict commissioned the construction of a cross that was to be hung over the emperor's gate to commemorate Christian martyrs.

That's remarkable.

Imagine going back in time and attempting to convince first-century Christians living in Rome that in the future the Colosseum would be dedicated to the suffering of their Lord. That the cross would come to symbolize life, not death. Love, not hate. Salvation, not suffering. Imagine the looks on their faces when you told them that the empire that crucified their Lord would one day embrace him as Lord. An imperial and cultural shift of that magnitude would have been impossible for them to imagine.

But it happened.

Could change of that magnitude happen again? In our nation?

Yes. But not the way we're currently going about it.

The tools and tactics of the kingdoms of this world will never bring about a revival of the kingdom of God.

Back to Bart.

After taking readers on a fascinating and informative tour of church history, Ehrman closes his book *The Triumph of Christianity* with an astonishing and honest assessment.

> Christianity not only took over an empire, it radically altered the lives of those living in it. . . . It was a revolution that affected government practices, legislation, art, literature, music, philosophy, and—on the even more fundamental level—the very understanding of billions of people about what it means to be human. However one evaluates the merits of the case, whether the Christianization of the West was a triumph to be treasured or a defeat to be lamented, no one can deny it was the *most monumental cultural transformation our world has ever seen.*[1]

Once more with feeling:

> Christianity was the catalyst for "the most monumental cultural transformation our world has ever seen."

Can it happen again?

That's up to us.

"Andy, don't you mean it's up to God?"

No. It's up to us.

God did his part. Jesus was unambiguous. We've got everything we need. We're already wearing the ruby slippers. History can repeat itself. And it should be easier this time around.

There are a lot more of us, and we have indoor plumbing.

But we have something else as well. Something working against us. We have an internalized, individualized, in-it-to-win-it version of Christianity that neither Jesus nor the apostle Paul would have recognized.

Actually, it's difficult for anybody to recognize.

(NOT SO) SELF-EVIDENT

Jordan Peterson, in *12 Rules for Life*, echoes Ehrman's observations:

> Christianity achieved the well-nigh impossible. The Christian doctrine elevated the individual soul, placing slave and master and commoner and nobleman alike on the same metaphysical footing, rendering them equal before God and the law. . . . The implicit transcendent worth of each and every soul established itself against impossible odds. . . . It is in fact nothing short of a *miracle* . . . that the hierarchical slave-based societies of our ancestors reorganized themselves,

under the sway of an ethical/religious revelation, such that the ownership and absolute domination of another person came to be viewed as wrong.[2]

His next statement is so instructive.

We forget that the opposite was *self-evident* throughout most of human history.[3]

Let's stop here for a moment.

Self-evident. As in, obvious, assumed, unquestioned.

When something is self-evident to one group, it's virtually impossible for that group to imagine that it's not equally self-evident to every other group. Why? Because it's self-evident! When something is self-evident, it hardly needs to be *stated*, much less *defended*.

In the ancient world, the virtue and morality of some people being owned by other people was self-evident. It was unquestioned. Aristotle, writing in the fourth century BC, summarized this ancient assumption as follows:

For that some should rule and others be ruled is a thing not only necessary, but expedient; from the hour of their birth, some are marked out for *subjection*, others for *rule* . . .[4]

What could be more obvious?

Slavery was just one of many ancient self-evident realities we modern folks find anything but. The superiority of men over women was self-evident, as was the double standard for men and women when it came to marital fidelity. Infanticide through exposure was self-evident as well. It was neither uncommon nor illegal for parents to abandon newborns on the banks of a river, on the edge of a forest, or outside the protective walls of a village. Babies were left to starve, freeze, or be eaten by wild animals.

Infanticide through exposure was not only legal in the Roman Empire, in certain circumstances it was considered an obligation. It wasn't considered murder because children didn't die because of something parents did. They died because of something parents didn't do. And it was possible that a child might actually survive—if the Fates chose to intervene. Either way, parents weren't culpable.

A letter dated June 17, 1 BC illustrates the detached indifference many ancients had toward newborns. The letter was written by a Roman soldier stationed in Alexandra to his wife.

Know that I am still in Alexandria; and do not worry if they [the army] wholly set out, I am staying in Alexandria. I ask you and entreat you, take care of the child, and if I receive my pay soon, I will send it up to you. Above all, if you bear a child and it is male, let it be; if it is female, cast it out.[5]

No discussion. No *wait till I get home and we'll decide together*. If it's a girl, expose it—and why not? Girls weren't as valuable as boys. A girl was just another mouth to feed.

To alter, much less reverse, a culturally held, self-evident assumption is no minor thing, especially when the assumption benefits the assumers. That Christianity—or as Peterson refers to it, "an ethical/religious revelation"—had the power to flip several ancient scripts is no small thing.

But—to the point of this book—how? Peterson gives us several clues:

> The society produced by Christianity was far less barbaric than the pagan—even the Roman—ones it replaced. . . . It objected to infanticide, to prostitution, and to the principle that might means right. It insisted that women were as valuable as men. . . . It demanded that even a society's enemies be regarded as human. . . . All of this was asking the impossible: but it happened.[6]

Indeed, it did. Nobody denies that it did.

Could something similar happen again?

Fun fact: In the fourth century, Saint Augustine, the famous Christian bishop from Hippo, declared that slavery was not, in fact, a *self-evident* by-product of the natural order. He declared it a by-product of sin! Decades earlier, with a bit of prompting from another Christian bishop,

Emperor Constantine declared infanticide a crime. Later, Emperor Valentinian made infanticide a capital offense.

This was a stunning imperial reversal that reflected a cultural shift in values, specifically the value of human life. A ritual practiced by parents for hundreds if not thousands of years in multiple cultures for reasons *so self-evident* that no one questioned it would henceforth be considered criminal.

What was the catalyst for the change?

The reversal happened in part because long before the value of a human life became *self-evident* to the Roman Empire, Christians were busy rescuing and raising abandoned children with no financial help from state and local governments. Christians rejected and condemned infanticide from the beginning. The Didache, a first-century Christian handbook, states, "You shall not . . . kill that which is born."[7] This sentiment was echoed by the church fathers. But early Christians took this mandate a step further. They visited the sites where children were commonly abandoned and took exposed children home to raise as their own.

Why?

Rescuing abandoned babies isn't commanded or even commended by Jesus or New Testament authors. Food was scarce and homes were small. Babies died all the time. Why would anyone put their own family at risk on behalf of an abandoned child? Refusing to expose your own children is one thing, but rescuing someone else's?

The Christian Scriptures didn't require it.

The Hebrew Scriptures didn't require it.

Something else required it.

Love.

Love required it.

Centuries before there were chapters and verses, Christians embraced real-world expressions of sacrificial love that eventually captured the attention of the empire and flipped multiple *self-evident* scripts.

And the world began to change.

THE KINGDOM COME NEAR

Philip Yancey, in his wonderful book *Vanishing Grace*, says this about the catalytic impact of the teaching of Jesus and the obedience of his first-century followers on the modern world.

> Those who condemn the church for its blind spots do so by gospel principles, arguing for the very moral values that the gospel originally set loose in the world.[8]

I love that phrase: ". . . set loose in the world." Jesus set something "loose in the world." Philip continues:

> Human rights, civil rights, women's rights, minority rights, gay rights, disability rights, animal rights—the

success of these modern movements reflects a wide-spread empathy for the oppressed that has no precedent in the ancient world.[9]

The reason there was no "widespread empathy for the oppressed" in the ancient world was, well, they didn't need a reason. It was *self-evident*. Ancients were Darwinian before Darwin.

> Classical philosophers considered mercy and pity to be character defects, contrary to justice. Not until Jesus did that attitude change.[10]

What is self-evident to us moderns was not self-evident anywhere in the world until Jesus. His others-first, everybody-matters value system set off a seismic cultural shift in Judea, Samaria, and eventually Rome. He came to the world not as prophet, priest, or religious figure. He came as king to establish a kingdom.

John the Baptist heralded Jesus's arrival. He drew enormous crowds to his desert sanctuary to hear a one-point sermon, a sermon that sent shock waves through the entire region:

> "Repent, for the kingdom of heaven has come *near*."[11]

How near?
Uncomfortably near.

And so it came to pass. Late one afternoon. As crowds lined the riverbank, waiting to be invited into the water. John stopped, smiled, pointed, and said,

"Look, the Lamb of God, who takes away the sin of the *world*!"[12]

This was the Lamb of God who came to make sense of this seemingly senseless, random world. This was a defining moment in history. Something new—someone new—had come. And with him, a kingdom. John tells us that Jesus immediately began proclaiming the "good news of God."[13]

"The time has come," [Jesus] said.[14]

The wait was over! Something was missing, but the time had arrived for what was missing to be missing no more. And what was missing?

"The kingdom of God has come *near*."[15]

The kingdom of God. The *reign* and *rule* of God. With the arrival of Jesus, God was extending his practical, real-world rule—his reign—beyond the borders of his covenant people, Israel. The kingdom was near because the King had come to town. Wherever the King goes, the kingdom goes with him. Jesus was not predicting a future event. His appearance was fulfillment. With the arrival of Jesus, God established his reign on earth in a new and unprecedented fashion. And everybody was invited to participate. This was the invitation:

"Repent and believe the good news!"[16]

We associate *repent* with turning away from something evil. Jesus was inviting his first-century audience to turn away from what, until that moment, was considered *self-evident*. Throughout his ministry, Jesus invited his audience to set aside their preconceived notions about the Father, one another, and the world in general. He invited them to something better. Something liberating.

He invited them to *believe* it. To *trust* it. To *center their lives around it*. In doing so, they would indeed be the light of the world because the Light had come to dwell in them. Lights would come on because the Light of the World had stepped into the room. The apostle John described it this way:

In him was life, and that life was the light of *all* mankind. The light shines in the darkness, and the darkness has *not overcome it*.[17]

John was an old man when he finally sat down to document his adventures with Jesus. When he wrote—or more than likely dictated—the words "the darkness has not overcome it," things were quite dark. Peter was dead. Paul was dead. Jerusalem and the surrounding region were being decimated by the Tenth Legion.

But amid so much darkness, the light of life was spreading like wildfire throughout the empire.

It would not be overcome.

It would overcome.

It would shape Western civilization.

KINGDOM COME

Jesus inaugurated an upside-down kingdom. A kingdom of the heart. A kingdom of conscience. A kingdom that would challenge and eventually flip the self-evident, self-centered scripts of the ancient world. In the end, he would voluntarily lay down his life for his subjects rather than demanding they lay down their lives for him. And he would require his followers to lay down their lives for one another.

That would be their distinctive. Their brand.

The Roman legions were efficient and merciless in their role as peace*keepers*. Jesus would instruct his followers to be peace*makers*.[18] In the end, he would serve as the ultimate peacemaker by making peace between the Father and his rebel race. His prodigal sons and daughters. His lost sheep. His misplaced coins. His enemies.

As citizens of the empire internalized and embraced the kingdom values Jesus introduced, the empire itself began to change. As a result, to quote Bart, the *ekklesia* of Jesus triggered *"the most monumental cultural transformation our world has ever seen."*[19]

But how?

How did a Judean cult birthed in the armpit of the empire, whose leader had been rejected by his own people and crucified by Rome, survive in the face of overwhelming resistance? How is it that this same upstart religion would eventually be embraced by the very empire that sought to extinguish it? Again, scholars and historians have pondered this mystery for generations. For the most part, they've all arrived at the same conclusion. British author Karen Armstrong sums it up this way: "Against all odds, by the third century, Christianity had become a force to be reckoned with. We still do not really understand how this came about."[20]

Humanly speaking, Karen is correct. It's undeniable, yet unexplainable. The role of scholars and historians, like medical doctors diagnosing a disease, is to look for natural causes. But when it comes to the unexplainable meteoric spread and influence of the church, perhaps we should simply accept the explanation offered by those closest to the actual events: the men and women who found themselves crushed between temple and empire.

What did they know that we don't?

What did they do that we won't?

Historically speaking, the Jesus movement should have been buried right alongside its founder.

But it wasn't.

The darkness did not overcome it.

Let's do that again.

CHAPTER FIVE

ON BRAND

Christians have attempted to bring about change in our nation through a variety of means. We've prayed and protested. We've boycotted brands, bands, and Disneyland. We've posted and tweeted. We've put signs in yards and waved signs on street corners. Basically, we've appropriated the techniques used by non-Christian folks on our side as well as folks on the other side. Their methods have become our methods. The way they broadcast their convictions is how we broadcast and market ours.

All of which would be fine if Jesus left it up to us to determine how to advance his movement. Further his kingdom. Represent his *ekklesia*. But he didn't.

Granted, most of the approaches available to us today weren't available in Jesus's day. But because of what he modeled and taught, I'm confident he would have passed up most of our novel—and ultimately ineffective—approaches to advancing his agenda. Not to mention, nation-*changing* was never part of his agenda. His agenda was broader than changing or rescuing any one nation.

His agenda encompassed *all* nations. Specifically, *people* from all nations.

SOMETHING NEW

Jesus didn't leave it up to us to determine how to advance his cause because his cause was and is unlike any other. Follow Jesus through the Gospels and it's unmistakably clear that he did not come to rebrand, repeat, or retread something old. Just the opposite. He came to introduce something entirely new. Brand-new. His uniquely new movement with its unique agenda called and calls for a unique export approach.

Jesus's unique personal claims, along with his unorthodox interpretation and application of the Torah, were unsettling for religious leaders. His teaching didn't fit *their* narrative. More disturbing, Jesus was wildly popular with Galileans as well as Judeans who lived outside Jerusalem. In the end, it was his popularity that brought divergent religious factions together to plot his arrest. If they couldn't recruit him and use him, the only other option was to get rid of him. With Rome's assistance, they did exactly that. For a few days.

Now one-third of the world's population worships him.

Apparently he knew what he was doing.

Perhaps we should hit pause on what we're doing and review his campaign strategy. He alluded to this strategy all along and made it uncomfortably clear on the night of his arrest.

NEW INDEED

When Judas slipped out to run his "errand," food was still on his plate. When the door closed behind him, it signaled the first in a series of events that would culminate in a nightmare for everyone in the room. They should have seen it coming. Jesus had warned them:

> "My children, I will be with you only a little longer. You will look for me, and just as I told the Jews, so I tell you now: Where I am going, you cannot come."[1]

Peter didn't hear anything after that. Jesus was leaving? Leaving the city? Leaving them *alone* in the city? That was a problem. Since entering Jerusalem, Jesus seemed to have gone out of his way to offend temple leaders. It was no secret they were plotting to arrest him. If he left town without them, they wouldn't be safe.

Then Jesus did what he often did. He changed the subject.

> "A new command I give you . . ."[2]

A new command?

They needed a new command like they needed—well, they didn't need a new command. What they needed was a plan. They were in Jerusalem during Passover. Jewish nationalism was at an all-time high. This was the annual commemoration and celebration of the nation's liberation from Egypt. No doubt first-century Jews had mixed emotions celebrating their ancestor's liberation from Egypt while occupied by Rome. Passover was an annual reminder of what God could do if only he would—namely, send another Moses or Joshua to expel the invaders. The men gathered with Jesus that evening hoped he was, in fact, Joshua 2.0. If that was the case, Passover would be the perfect time for Jesus to reveal his secret identity and get the kingdom party started.

Perhaps Judas's sudden disappearance had something to do with last-minute preparations for the big reveal.

But a new command?

The current list kept them plenty busy. Besides, earlier, Jesus had reduced the traditional list to two commands: love God and love your neighbor.[3] So why add a third? And why now? Besides, Moses was the command giver. Cataloging, classifying, prioritizing, and interpreting commands was one thing. Adding to them? Only God had the authority to add commands. Then again, only God had the authority to forgive sin.[4] Only God had the power to give sight to the blind. Or raise the dead.

Oh well.

Turns out Jesus wasn't adding a command to an existing list of commands. He was doing something far more radical than that. He continued:

"A new command I give you: Love one another . . ."[5]

That wasn't *new*. But Jesus wasn't *through*.

What came next was . . . blasphemous. What came next changed the world. What came next could change our neighborhoods, cities, and eventually our nation. It doesn't require signs, boycotts, or voter guides. It doesn't require praying for revival. If we embraced what came next, there would be a revival. What came next trumped the Golden Rule. I call it the platinum rule.

"As I have loved you, so you must love one another."[6]

That was new.

Doing for others what one hoped others would do for them in return was so . . . so old covenant. Jesus instructed his followers to do unto one another as *he* had done unto them.

This was personal.

This new brand of love was extraordinarily personal for the men seated around that table. When we read "Love as I have loved you," we think of the cross. They didn't. They thought back over the previous three years. Each man in the room could remember a moment when Jesus had loved him particularly well. He could have called 'em out one by one.

"Matthew, remember when we met?"

"Yes, Rabbi."

"Remember what you were doing?"

"Of course, Rabbi. Everybody remembers what I was doing. I used the authority of Rome as a cover to steal from my own people."

"Do you remember what I said to you?"

"Yes, Rabbi, you invited me to follow you. In those days people were nervous if they thought I was following them."

"Matthew, extend the same grace I extended to you to everyone you meet for the rest of your life. Love as I have loved you!"

"Nathanael, remember the day we met? Remember what you said about me? 'Can anything good come from Nazareth?' You dissed my town, my family, my childhood friends. But I invited you anyway. Extend that same grace and forgiveness to everybody you meet. As I have loved you . . ."

One by one, Jesus could have taken each of them back to a moment in their shared history and reminded them of the patience, kindness, and grace he had extended to them in spite of their fear, insecurity, and doubt.

But he didn't stop there.

The significance of what Jesus said next cannot be overstated. As circumcision was the distinguishing mark for a man included in the old covenant, so this new-command, one-another brand of love would be the mark of any man or woman who chose to participate in Jesus's new covenant. New-command-brand love was to serve as the unifying, identifying mark of his *ekklesia*. His new command—to love as he loved—would be the governing ethic, the standard against which all behavior was to be measured for those who called him Lord. And this new command was to be applied first and foremost to those who claimed Jesus as Lord.

> "By *this* everyone will know that you are my disciples . . ."[7]

The term *this* is a demonstrative pronoun. Remember those? Demonstrative pronouns are used to point to something specific. In this case, it's a *singular* demonstrative pronoun. Jesus submitted one specific behavior that was to be *the* identifying characteristic of his followers.

> "By this everyone will know that you are my disciples, if you *love* one another."[8]

How we treat, talk about, respond to, and care for one another is the identifying mark of a genuine Jesus follower.

Not what we believe.

Nobody knows and nobody is better off because of what we believe.

Doing makes the difference. Doing changed the world. Love, as Jesus defined it, for one another is our differentiator, which means our love for one another should be noticeable, notable, and distinct. According to Jesus, anyway. The new-covenant brand of love Jesus calls us to is neither easy nor natural. That's what makes it noticeable, notable, and distinct.

Theologian Don Carson writes, "I suspect that one of the reasons why there are so many exhortations in the New Testament for Christians to love other Christians is because this is not an easy thing to do."[9] He continues:

> Ideally, however, the church itself is not made up of natural "friends." It is made up of natural enemies. What binds us together is not common education, common race, common income levels, common politics, common nationality, common accents, common jobs, or anything else of that sort. Christians come together, not because they form a natural collocation, but because they have all been saved by Jesus Christ and owe him a common allegiance.[10]

This next statement is gold:

> In the light of this common allegiance, in the light of the fact that they have all been loved by Jesus himself, they commit themselves to doing what he says—and he commands them to love one another. In this light, they are a band of natural enemies who love one another for Jesus' sake.[11]

I know. You've heard this before. And it's so naive. So simplistic. It's not how the game is played. It's not how the world works. It's not how progress is made. Love isn't a *winning* strategy.

Perhaps not.

But so what?

I'm not the one suggesting that Jesus's new-covenant command should govern our behavior, responses, language, and tone.

Jesus is.

The Jesus in whose name you pray when your child is sick, when your marriage is in jeopardy, or when you hit a bump financially. That Jesus, the Jesus who has your undivided attention when tragedy strikes.

If we think his new-covenant command sounds impractical, weak, passive, and ineffectual, imagine how it sounded to the group gathered with him that evening for Passover. When they entered Jerusalem a few days earlier, they entered the lion's den. The empire and the temple held all the cards. Their opponents had all the power. They controlled the crowd—by force if necessary. And the best Jesus could come up with was . . .

"As I have loved you, so you must love one another."[12]

Seriously, Jesus? That's all you got?

If word of this insidious, subversive, empire-threatening plot reached Rome, Tiberius Caesar wouldn't sleep for weeks! If Caiaphas caught wind of what Jesus and his disciples were plotting in the upper room that evening, he and his cronies would have fled the city!

We're doomed!
Escape while you can!
They're going to love one another!

Quick reminder: The Roman Forum is now a tourist attraction, and the remains of Herod's Temple are scattered around the base of its ancient walls.

Apparently Jesus was on to something.

PRACTICAL AND POLITICAL

Quick question.

Is there a notable difference between Republican Jesus followers and Republican *non*-Jesus followers? Is there a noticeable difference between Democrats who follow Jesus and Democrats who don't?

While you're thinking, here's what I think.

No. Generally speaking, there is no discernable public difference. You've never heard anyone in media or culture make that distinction. Worse, you rarely hear Republicans or Democrats who consider themselves Jesus followers make or draw attention to that distinction. But it would be easy to do if national leaders were more committed to their faith than their political party.

"So, Senator, do you agree with the vice president's comments regarding House member Gleason's decision?"

"Well, I agree with the vice president's position, but as a follower of Jesus, I do not support the language used by the vice president or the mischaracterization and oversimplification of House member Gleason's position. Like me, House member Gleason is also a Christian. We have far more in common than not."

That would be noticeable, notable, and newsworthy. Back to Jesus.

SUBTLE, SIGNIFICANT

Jesus's new command involved a subtle but significant departure from precedent that I assume was lost on the apostles that night. After all, there was a lot going on.

Jesus didn't tether his new command to the anchor all Jewish commands were traditionally tethered to: love for, fear of, or dedication to God. Jesus tethered his new command to *himself*. He inserted himself into an equation mere mortals have no business inserting themselves into. His new command represented a not-so-subtle shift from vertical to horizontal. The litmus test for being a card-carrying Jesus follower involved nothing even remotely religious. It was relational. It had nothing to do with how one treated God. It had everything to do with how one treated others.

Following Jesus didn't require looking for ways to get closer to God, who dwelled out there, up there, somewhere.

Jesus followers would demonstrate their devotion to God by putting the person *next* to them in *front* of them. It was a one-another way of life.

But the shift didn't stop there.

Conspicuously missing from Jesus's new-command instructions was any reference to his *divine* right to require such allegiance and obedience. In what was arguably his most future-defining set of instructions, Jesus refused to play the God card. Even in this final, if-you-forget-everything-else-I've-said-remember-this exchange, Jesus did not leverage his holiness, his personal righteousness, his moral authority, or his supernatural abilities.

Jesus leveraged his *example*—how he loved.[13]

Think about that.

Jesus's love for the people in the room, rather than his authority over the people in the room, is what he leveraged to instruct and inspire the people in the room. He refused to exercise his power in the traditional ways power is exercised by powerful people.

Why?

Because he was introducing something new. Something that included a new paradigm for how power was to be used and leveraged. Jesus was not anti-power or anti-privilege. In the end, he would declare the scope of his power, which was rooted in his privilege:

All authority in heaven and on earth has been given to me.[14]

He did not deny or downplay his privileged standing with the Father. He spoke of it on so many occasions, his enemies used it against him. But unlike the powerful and privileged civil and religious leaders of his day, Jesus refused to leverage his privilege and power for his own sake. He flipped that script. And during that final Passover meal, he required his followers to do the same.

And they got the message.

They got the message in part because during that same gathering, he demonstrated his new kingdom ethic in the most awkward and uncomfortable way imaginable. He washed their feet.

After the resurrection, Jesus shared something with John that John included in his account of the events that transpired that evening. Something that places this famous incident in a context far beyond the realm of politeness and poor Passover planning. This is John's introduction to this epic piece of history:

> Jesus knew that the Father had put all things *under his power*, and that he had come from God and was returning to God.[15]

"All things were under his power."

In that moment, Jesus understood that his Father had given him authority over all things. All people. All events. He could call the shots. He could call off the events planned for the following day.

So what do you do . . . what do I do . . . when we realize *we've got the power?* We've got the *position.* We've got the *privilege.*

Here's what Jesus did:

> He got up from the meal, took off his outer clothing, and wrapped a *towel* around his waist. After that, he poured water into a basin and began to wash his disciples' feet, drying them with the towel that was wrapped around him.[16]

> When he had finished washing their feet, he put on his clothes and returned to his place and said,

Who was in charge of organizing this event?

Actually . . .

> "You call me 'Teacher' and 'Lord,' and rightly so, for that is what I am."[17]

Implication: I've got the power, privilege, and authority.

> "Now that I, your Lord and Teacher, have washed your feet, you also should wash *one another's* feet. I have set you an example that you should *do* as I *have done* for you. Very truly I tell you, no servant

is greater than his master, nor is a messenger greater than the one who sent him. Now that you know these things, you will be blessed if you *do* them."[18]

How should Jesus-following Republicans and Democrats treat, speak about, and respond to one another? Publicly and privately? The way Jesus treated, spoke to, and responded to those who disagreed with him.

Unless, of course, we think we're greater than our Lord. If we do, we should tell him.

Actually, we don't need to tell him.

He knows.

Our unwillingness to be kind to, pray for, serve, honor, and speak respectfully to and about those we differ with politically is evidence that we, in fact, consider ourselves greater than our Master.

Until there's an emergency.

Then we're hands up, knees to the floor, surrendered and willing to do anything.

Later that evening, Jesus and his band of brothers would suffer disappointment, defeat, and defection. Empire and temple came together to conspire against them. Love wasn't enough. So they lost. By every political calculation—ancient and modern—Jesus lost.

Jesus refused to deploy his resources for his own benefit. He refused to employ the tactics used so effectively by the kingdoms of this world. He had come to do the will of his

Father. And even with the knowledge that all authority had been given to him, he stuck to the plan.

He lost.

This does not sit well with me. It's not very American. I like to win. We're wired to win. Turns out Jesus was not against winning. Turns out he was playing a completely different game with a different set of rules and, consequently, a different definition for *winning*.

Jesus played to lose so the other team could win. Jesus played to lose so sinners like you could win. So sinners like me had a chance. And a second chance. And a third. Then he extended an invitation to those of us who won because he lost:

"Follow me."[19]

Impractical?

Yes.

No.

It depends on how you define *winning*.

Jesus didn't anchor his new command to his divine right as king. He anchored it to his sacrificial love. Why should his disciples obey his command to love? Because he loved them first. He loved them best. And then he instructed them to do unto others as he had done, and was about to do, unto them.

The following afternoon, Jesus staged a demonstration

of love that took their breath away. A demonstration of love that took their sin away. But it took something else away as well. Their excuses.

When they understood the length to which Jesus was willing to go to demonstrate love for friends and enemies alike, they lost every conceivable excuse not to embrace and embody his new-covenant marching orders.

To love as he loved.

Regardless.

"By this everyone will know that you are my disciples, if you love one another."[20]

SOMEONE NOTICED

The New Testament book of Acts documents the explosive growth of the Jesus movement following his resurrection. Within months, the movement was embraced by Judeans, Samaritans, Galileans, and Roman citizens. Thanks to the tireless efforts of the apostle Paul and others, the movement gained followers in centers of commerce throughout the Mediterranean basin. Unfortunately, the impact of the church on Greek and Roman culture in the years following the death of the apostles is a story with which most Christians are unfamiliar. It's an extraordinarily important bit of history for several reasons, not the least of which was the cultural shift that transpired in subsequent decades and made possible the creation of the Bible.

But the impact of the early church on culture is as instructive as it is interesting. It's instructive in that it explains how this Nazarene cult caught in the crosshairs of empire and temple outlived one and shaped the culture and worldview of the other. As stated earlier, no one disputes that it happened. The question is how. The history of the church in the decades following the death of the apostles documents the answer to that question. It tells us *how* they did it.

And how did they do it?

The short answer is that they did what Jesus instructed them to do. They adopted Jesus's new-covenant command as a way of life. It wasn't a reference point. It was the context for everything. Most noticeable, it informed their response to suffering—theirs as well as the suffering of people around them. The Jesus movement was characterized by uncharacteristic compassion, generosity, selflessness, and boldness. Boldness not born of arrogance but fueled by confidence. Boldness fueled by concern for those who had not yet heard the good news of what God had done on behalf of the world.

Rodney Stark, Michael Walsh, and Alvin J. Schmidt, among others, have documented the unprecedented compassion that characterized Christians in the second and third centuries.[21] Doing good for someone who was not able to do good for you in return was not considered virtuous in Greek and Roman culture. It was considered foolish, a passion indulged by weak-willed women. But Christians considered no-strings-attached generosity the epitome of virtue. It was a noticeable and noteworthy way of fulfilling Christ's new-covenant command. It was a tangible way of loving others as Christ had loved.

And so, against unimaginable odds, the Jesus movement spread to the very heart of the Roman Empire. By the beginning of the second century, it had captured the attention of pagans both inside and outside that empire. One of those pagans was a lawyer turned Christian theologian and apologist named Quintus Septimius Florens Tertullianus, better known as Tertullian. Tertullian was both a product of as well as an eyewitness to the spread of Christianity in the late second and early third centuries. While studying in Rome, Tertullian met his first Christians. They impressed him with their devotion, courage, compassion, and morality. He was fascinated as well by their belief in a single deity. Eventually he joined one of the expanding networks of house churches in the city and in time rose to prominence as a fierce defender of the faith. When Tertullian penned the following words, crosses in Rome still had bodies hanging from them. Yet the *ekklesia* of Jesus flourished. Here's his description:

> What shall I say of the Romans themselves, who fortify their own empire with garrisons of their own legions, nor can extend the might of their kingdom beyond these nations? But Christ's Name is extending everywhere, believed everywhere, worshipped by all

the above enumerated nations, reigning everywhere, adored everywhere, conferred equally everywhere upon all. No king, with Him, finds greater favor, no barbarian lesser joy; no dignities or pedigrees enjoy distinctions of merit; to all He is equal, to all King, to all Judge, to all God and Lord.[22]

"But Christ's name is extending everywhere, believed everywhere . . ."

Extending everywhere.

But how?

By being Christian.

Not our version of Christian. The Antioch version of Christian. They were living out Jesus's new-covenant command. I should point out that when Tertullian penned those words, not only did Roman crosses still have bodies hanging from them, but the first Bible wouldn't be assembled for another 150 years. But even without an agreed upon or accessible text, the influence of the church continued to spread.

THE GODS MUST BE ANGRY

In his most famous work, *Apologeticus*, Tertullian summarizes the posture of the empire toward the expansion of Christianity in the second century:

If the Tiber reaches the walls, if the Nile does not rise to the fields,

> if the sky does not move or the earth does, if there
>   is famine,
> if there is plague, they cry at once,
> "The Christians to the lions!"[23]

In short, Christians were blamed for pretty much everything.

Why?

Where Christianity increased, sacrifices to the gods decreased. When sacrifices decreased, the gods were angry! When the gods were angry, bad things happened.

The solution?

Rid the empire of the atheist Christians.

You read that correctly. Christians were considered atheists in the second and third centuries. They didn't believe in gods.

Like the Jews, Christians believed there was only one God. Unlike the Jews, Christians weren't given a pass. Christianity was a *new* superstition. Judaism traced its roots back to the beginning. The beginning as in, "In the beginning God . . ."[24] You can't go much further back than that. Rome esteemed ancient things. So the empire granted Jews a special exemption. Jews did not have to swear allegiance to or sacrifice to Caesar. In exchange, priests in Jerusalem were required to offer up daily prayers on behalf of Caesar. But Christians, even Jewish converts to Christianity, were not exempt.

ASSISTANCE REQUIRED

Early in the second century, during the rule of Emperor Trajan, the empire experienced a series of setbacks—interpreted to mean that the gods weren't happy. Emperor Trajan needed somebody to blame. So he issued an edict instructing governors throughout the empire to arrest and imprison the Christians in their communities.

Pliny the Younger, a relative of the emperor and governor of a province located in modern-day Turkey, was eager to please his boss. But Pliny found the edict confusing and incomplete. The emperor's edict didn't include the specific crime Christians were to be charged with. And there were no instructions for how they were to be punished or to what degree they could be "investigated"—Roman speak for *tortured*.

In an effort to gain a bit more direction, Pliny wrote the emperor a letter. But before sending his letter, he did a bit of investigating on his own. Pliny arrested a handful of Christians and brought them in for questioning. The following is what he discovered and included in his report to the emperor.

What he discovered is why I included this story:

> The sum and substance of their fault or error had been that they were accustomed to meet on a fixed day before dawn and sing responsively a hymn to Christ as to a god.[25]

No schemin'. Just singin'. In Pliny's time, Christians met on Sunday mornings before dawn. Why so early? There were no weekends. Sunday was the first day of the workweek. Christians met before work. Imagine what would happen to church attendance if we met on Mondays before work.

During these clandestine early-morning meetings, they would sing. Why sing? They had very little, if any, written literature. Hymns were the primary means by which Christian theology was rehearsed and remembered.

Back to Pliny:

They were accustomed to meet on a fixed day before dawn . . . and to bind themselves by oath, not to some crime, but . . .[26]

Now, this next part is the best part. Every Sunday morning, Christians would gather and recommit themselves to a specific code of conduct that reflected the new-covenant command of Jesus:

. . . not to some crime, but *not to commit fraud, theft, or adultery, not falsify their trust, nor to refuse to return a trust when called upon to do so.*[27]

Sounds like a dangerous bunch.

This discovery left Governor Pliny with a dilemma. The Christians in his province were the best citizens in his province! They were notably and noticeably better citizens than the average Jupiter-worshiping Roman for whom adultery and the deceit that went along with it were standard fare. But since the emperor was convinced Christians were a threat, perhaps Pliny was missing something. Perhaps the Christians he questioned weren't telling the truth. So Pliny took his investigation a step further. Fortunately for us, what he did next was also included in his letter to the emperor.

> I judged it all the more necessary to find out what the truth was by torturing two female slaves who were called deaconesses. But I discovered nothing else but depraved, excessive superstition.[28]

Superstition in all likelihood was a reference to the resurrection. He continues:

> I have never participated in trials of Christians. I therefore do not know what offenses it is the practice to punish or investigate, and to what extent.[29]

Governor Pliny wasn't sure what he was supposed to be looking for. Up to that point, he hadn't found anything deserving of punishment, much less execution.

Sound familiar?

> Then Pilate announced to the chief priests and the crowd, "I find no basis for a charge against this man."[30]

Apparently, second-century Jesus followers were actually . . . following Jesus. It didn't hurt that the apostle Paul directly addressed believers' conduct among unbelievers.

> Make it your ambition to lead a quiet life: You should *mind your own business* and work with your hands, just as we told you, so that your daily life may win the respect of *outsiders*.[31]

When's the last time you heard a sermon on *minding your own business*? Apparently second-century Jesus followers understood how to mind their own business in a way that made people curious about the business they were minding. They were so curious, they eventually embraced this new "superstition." Here's how Pliny wraps up his report to the emperor.

> I therefore postponed the investigation and hastened to consult you. For the matter seemed to me to warrant consulting you, especially because . . .

Don't miss this.

> . . . especially because of the *number* involved. For *many* persons of every age, every rank, and also of both sexes are and will be endangered. For the contagion of this superstition has spread not only to the cities but also to the villages and farms.[32]

I love that.

Let's do that again.

Let's make Christianity *contagious* again.

Our first-, second-, and third-century brothers and sisters captured the attention of their pagan neighbors through their character, morality, work ethic, and friendship. These fine men and women were guilty of meeting together on a fixed day before dawn, singing a hymn to Christ, and committing to honesty, generosity, fidelity, and loyalty to one another and anyone else who needed a favor.

Less than three generations after the resurrection, so many Roman citizens embraced this new "superstition" that a Roman governor was concerned about the number of arrests he would have to make if required to arrest everyone associated with these unusual gatherings. In his words, "For the contagion of this superstition has spread not only to the cities but also to the villages and farms."[33]

It's everywhere!

And not only aren't they doing anything wrong, they recommit themselves once a week to do everything right.

Governor Pliny received a response from Emperor Trajan.

You observed proper procedure, my dear Pliny, in sifting the cases of those who had been denounced to you as Christians. For it is not possible to lay down any general rule to serve as a kind of fixed standard.

They are not to be sought out; if they are denounced and proved *guilty*, they are to be punished, with this reservation, that whoever denies that he is a Christian and really proves it—that is, by *worshipping our gods*—even though he was under suspicion in the past, shall obtain pardon through *repentance*.[34]

Early Christians were not despised for their behavior. They were despised by the empire for their allegiance to Christ. Imagine if that were the only legitimate charge that could be leveled against us.

The problem with Christians is that they love their *Savior* more than they love their country!

We've lost our voice and diminished our influence because for too many of us the opposite is true. I'm not suggesting that you love your country less. I'm suggesting that we love one another better. In doing so we demonstrate our allegiance to our Savior, who made it clear that our love for one another is the best evidence of our love for the Father.

If we want to make America great, we should make more great citizens, citizens for whom

the sum and substance of their fault or error is that they are accustomed to meet on a fixed day and sing responsively a hymn to Christ as to a god and to bind themselves by oath, not to some crime, but not to commit fraud, theft, or adultery, not falsify their trust, nor to refuse to return a trust when called upon to do so.[35]

If we want to make America great, we should follow the example of those first-century Christians in Turkey. We should gather every week and rededicate ourselves to our Savior and to one another. We should take an oath to be model citizens. Model employers and employees. Faithful husbands and wives. In the words of the apostle Paul, we should live lives that win the respect of outsiders. We should love one another the way God through Christ loved us. And if we run out of ideas, we should go look for some feet to wash.

And again, second-century Christians didn't have a Bible. Which means we twenty-first-century Christians don't have any excuses.

ONCE UPON A TIME

Once upon a time, the love-one-another culture of the church stood in sharp contrast to the bite-and-devour-one-another culture of the pagan world. In a society that valued conquest and the consolidation of power above all things, the teaching of Jesus was judged as weak, feminine, pathetic. By every ancient standard, the God worshiped by Christians lost. He was defeated. He was executed by his enemies. Worse, he surrendered himself to be executed. The odds of this knockoff Judean sect gaining traction was, well, it wasn't going to happen.

But it did.

What struck the ancient world initially as pathetic and appalling eventually came to be seen as inviting and appealing. In the end, it was contagious. So contagious that it infected the empire dedicated to its demise.

Against all odds, a cult dedicated to a crucified teacher with no territory, military, or recognized authority survived, multiplied, and eventually replaced the prevailing . . . not religion. Christianity replaced the prevailing worldview.

When the Jesus movement was fueled and informed by his new-covenant command, it was neither pathetic nor weak. It was unprecedented. It was unstoppable.

It was notable and noticeable.

It was, well, it was pretty much everything we collectively have ceased to be.

It was what we must become once again.

Doing so will not require political alignment or a new political movement. It will require something far more demanding. It will require us to step back onto the original foundation of our faith. It will require us to embrace the new-covenant ethic Jesus introduced and illustrated. It will require us to love one another.

Not in our hearts.

It will require us to love one another on both sides of the political aisle with our words and with our deeds, with our social media posts, our responses, our resources, and our sermons. It will require us to stop sizing people up and writing them off because of their political views. To do anything less is to declare through our actions that we are *greater* than our Master.

We've protested and boycotted. We've posted and tweeted. We've called people out. We've called people names. We've stereotyped. Shamed. Blamed. We've taken sides. We've politicized our churches.

What if we took a break from all that and tried this:

"A new command I give you: Love one another. As I have loved you, so you must love one another. By this everyone will know that you are my disciples, if you love one another."[36]

That's the way forward. It's not complicated. It's costly, but it's not complicated. That's how it's done. That's how it *was* done. Let's do that again.

CHAPTER SIX

ONE FOR THE WIN

We know it's possible for Christians to disagree politically. But is it possible for us to disagree politically without disrupting our *unity*?

Jesus thought so. But it won't be easy. Here's one reason why: fundamental attribution error. Whether you've heard of it or not, you've certainly experienced it. Fundamental attribution error describes our tendency to attribute people's behavior to their *character*, while attributing our behavior to our *circumstances*.

When your coworker, who you don't really like, is late to a meeting, you assume he's disorganized, lacks a strong work ethic, and is probably not all that concerned about the success of your team. After all, how hard is it to be on time?

But when you're late?

When you're late, it is 100 percent circumstantial. Traffic. Crisis at home. You may go so far as to assume your reputation as a responsible employee is so airtight that you don't even need to explain your late arrival. Your associates will assume it's the result of *circumstances* beyond your control.

Fundamental attribution error happens when we assume someone's actions reflect the kind of person they are rather than circumstances they're navigating. It's easy to see how this error affects us at home and at work. But it affects us politically as well.

"The corrupt Democrats."

"The mindless Republicans."

"Clearly, something is wrong with these people. How can they say that? How can they support her? How could they vote for him?"

Thanks to fundamental attribution error, we know the answer to those questions. It's because Democrats are godless socialists and Republicans are ignorant racists. The Democrats want to flood the nation with illegals, and Republicans are only concerned about preserving their wealth. The political views held by those on the other side don't have anything to do with how they grew up, where they grew up, who they grew up around, or what they experienced along the way. They aren't responding to circumstances and experiences. They have a character problem.

Fundamental attribution error is everywhere—cable news, Twitter, Facebook, your inbox. Pew Research Center reported in 2019 that 55 percent of Republicans and 47 percent of Democrats view members of the other party as more immoral than average Americans.[1] According to a more recent survey, the percentage of Americans who "strongly dislike" the opposition party has gone up 400 percent over the past two decades.[2] While the stats are discouraging, the real-world consequences could be disastrous. Fundamental attribution error divides us. It divides us with a lie. Justin Giboney, political strategist and founder of the AND Campaign, explains: "One ugly reality about hating your political opponents is that you start off hating their vices and end up hating their virtues as well. In your contempt, you begin to believe that everything about them is wrong, even their insights and practices that could improve you."[3]

Mature, emotionally intelligent, curious, empathetic people don't fall for it.

Jesus followers shouldn't fall for it either.

There's too much at stake.

James, the brother of Jesus, reminds us that we are to be *quick* to listen and *slow* to speak.[4] Slow to form judgments. Slow to allow other people to form our judgments. Instead of forming uninformed opinions or perpetuating one-dimensional caricatures, we are to take cues from our Savior, who surrounded himself with all kinds of people. Real people. Complex people. People like you. Like me.

So, one more time: We know it's possible for Christians to disagree politically. But can we disagree politically without disrupting our *unity*?

Again, yes. But it will require something of us. Something we briefly touched on in chapter 3. To disagree politically and maintain our unity will require us to evaluate our politics through the filter of our faith rather than the other way around. Which, of course, is something we're all convinced we're already doing. We're on the Lord's side and he supports our side. And the people on the other side who are deluded into thinking the Lord is on their side need to switch sides.

So what's going on?

Not what's going on with you.

You've got it right.

I mean, what's going on with those Christians in the *other* party? How can they even call themselves Christians and support those policies and those candidates?

While those questions may be good and important ones, they don't advance the conversation.

So let's try a different question.

Are you willing to follow Jesus if doing so requires you to reject portions of your party's platform?

To take it a step further, are you willing to speak up when following Jesus puts you at odds with the views, the tone, or the decisions of your party or your party's candidate of choice? Locally or nationally?

We all know the correct answer. But now you're suspicious. This feels like a setup. Feels like a gotcha is just a page or two away. But I already gotcha. I gotcha to read the first five chapters of this book.

Anyway.

The second question is more difficult to answer honestly because it's potentially dangerous relationally. It may be professionally dangerous as well. It's difficult and potentially dangerous because in the current political climate, *disagreement* is *defection*. There's no middle ground. But if we're unwilling to compromise *politically*, we will compromise our faith *eventually*.

We won't compromise what we *believe*. We'll compromise our faith in other, more subtle ways.

Since the fourth century, the church has gone to great lengths to create its own version of the pagan divide between sacred and secular. Animal sacrifice to appease the gods has been replaced with belief and doctrine. When we were children, we were encouraged to accept Jesus as our Savior, not our king. It was enough to believe. But you don't find that in the Gospels or among the brave activists who turned the world upside down before the first Bible was assembled. The first Bible was assembled because the world had been turned upside down.

Reducing Christianity to a set of static belief statements provides believers on both sides of the aisle with an escape hatch. An excuse hatch. Reducing Christianity to beliefs makes syncing our faith with a political platform effortless. It's why there are Christians on both sides of the political aisle. Believers *believe* pretty much the same things. But our political convictions come in all shapes, sizes, and colors.

But follow Jesus though the Gospels and you'll discover

that the kingdom he introduced and invited us to participate in is a kingdom characterized by *public behavior*, not *private belief*. What he never said is as instructive as what he did. Jesus never said,

> By *this* everyone will know that you are my disciples,
> if you *believe* correctly.

The world will know whose we are and whose kingdom we represent by how we treat, respond to, serve, forgive, and talk about one another.

Do you know how many times the term *faith* appears in the Sermon on the Mount?

Exactly *one* time.

The Sermon on the Mount is not a treatise on what Jesus followers should *believe*. It's a vision cast for how we should *behave*, how we should *respond*, and what to expect along the way. Here's an uncomfortable excerpt:

> "You have heard that it was said, 'Love your neighbor and hate your enemy.'"[5]

Did anyone really need to say that? Common sense, right? Kingdoms of this World 101.

> "But I tell you, love your enemies and pray for those who persecute you."[6]

Do you *do* that? We all *believe* we should do that. But do we? Do you?

Odds are, your theology, your belief system, is buttoned up and proof-texted in place. It aligns perfectly with your politics. But do you *actively* love, serve, and bear the burdens of people who aren't like you and who disagree with you? Do you *pray* for anybody on the other side of the political aisle? Pray *for*. Not at. Not against. The Greek term is ὑπέρ. It means on behalf of. Do you pray on their behalf?

What comes next is, well, it would be inspiring if it weren't so confusing.

> ". . . that you may be *children* of your Father in heaven."[7]

The church reduced becoming a child of God to *believing* something. Jesus didn't. Jesus equates it with *doing* something. According to Jesus, our heavenly Father would like for us to *behave* like him, not just *believe* in him.

Here's one more.

> "If you love those who love you, what reward will you get? Are not even the *tax collectors* doing that?"[8]

Even Democrats do that!
Republicans do that!
Middle schoolers do that!
If you're a Jesus follower, it's not enough to *do that*.

We won't be notable if we just do that. Loving people who can love us back is what the other party does. It's what everybody does. Again, it's Kingdoms of this World 101.

My point?

As long as we're content to be *believers* rather than *doers*, we will be *divided*.

Reducing faith to a list of beliefs provides us with plenty of margin not to love, forgive, provide for, celebrate, and pray for people we disagree with. Reducing faith to a list of beliefs frees us to slander people we don't align with politically. It gives us license to mock, jeer, and celebrate the failure of people whose views differ from ours. If your version of Christianity leaves the door open to those behaviors, you're nothing like your Father in heaven. And you're nothing like his Son.

You are an instrument of *disunity*.

You are working for the *enemy*.

You are contributing to the very thing Jesus prayed we would avoid. If someone's political views make their feet too dirty for you to wash, you can be sure your politics are informing and deforming your faith. We cannot reduce membership in God's kingdom to *belief*, because the King doesn't allow it.

> "Let your *light* shine before others, that they may see your good *deeds* and glorify your Father in heaven."[9]

As long as we're content to be *believers* rather than *doers,* we will be *divided*. Our politics will divide us.

Again, we will be reduced to a constituency rather than the conscience of the nation and the light of the world.

HE MUST HAVE SEEN IT COMING

Unity doesn't come naturally. Division comes naturally. "What's in it for me" comes naturally. Unity with people like me—that comes naturally. Unity with people unlike me? Who may not *like* me? Who has time for that? There's no incentive for me to make time for that. Why go out of my way for something so difficult and unnecessary?

Jesus saw this coming. He saw *us* coming. So he prayed for us.

> "My prayer is not for *them* alone. I pray also for *those* who will believe in me through their message."[10]

Them being the apostles. *Those* being us.

Before we dive into what Jesus prayed for, what do you pray for?

I already know.

You pray for the same things I tend to pray for. We pray for what's most important to us. So most of our prayers revolve around . . . *us*. And the people who mean the most to *us*. If you want to know what's most important to you, look at your credit card statements and your calendar and listen to your prayers. If you want to know what was most important to Jesus, listen to his prayers. If what was most important to Jesus is not most important, or at least some-what important, to us . . . we're probably not followers. Users perhaps. But not followers.

The one thing Jesus prayed *for us* is one thing very few of us pray for at all, which indicates that it's just not that important *to* us. *Us* who are convinced we believe correctly. *Us* who are confident that our faith informs our politics.

Of all the things Jesus could have prayed when he prayed for the future church, why did he choose what he chose? He chose what he chose because it was mission critical. It was an essential ingredient. No amount of anything else would compensate for it. It was the sugar in the sugar cookies. The banana in the banana split.

If you're familiar with Jesus's prayer in John 17, you know what I'm referring to. If you aren't—and my hunch is, most believers aren't—well, that's part of the problem. So here it is, hours before his arrest, weeks before he handed his enterprise off to the eleven remaining apostles. This was Jesus's greatest concern. This was his prayer request.

Jesus . . . looked toward heaven and prayed:

"Father, the hour has come. Glorify your Son, that your Son may glorify you."[11]

The hour in which God was most *glorified*, we would have been most *horrified*. We would have looked away.

But God never looked better. Jesus was referring to the events of the following day. The hour that would change everything. The hour that by every human indicator would indicate that Jesus lost. Speaking of himself, he continues:

"For you granted him authority over all people that he might give eternal life to all those you have given him."[12]

Then Jesus defines eternal life. No mention of heaven. Just a relationship with the Father and his Son.

"Now this is eternal life: that they know you, the only true God, and Jesus Christ, whom you have sent."[13]

Then he points to the shared, communal "work" that he and the Father had been working as *one* throughout Jesus's ministry.

"I have brought you glory on earth by finishing the *work* you gave me to do."[14]

What was that work? To reveal what the Father was like to a handful of followers who would in turn distribute that knowledge to the world. Then Jesus asks that his work, the work of revealing the Father to the world, would continue uninterrupted through the apostles.

"Protect them by the power of your name, the name you gave me, so that *they may be one* as we are *one*."[15]

By *one*, Jesus is not referring to a paranormal, transcendental state. He's referring to the joint mission that he and the Father had been cooperating on since his introduction by John the Baptist. Jesus is asking that this joint venture would continue with and through his apostles. That just as he and the Father were in lockstep with each other, so the apostles would be as well.

Notice that Jesus prays for their protection—but not their physical protection. He's asking the Father to protect them from becoming anything other than one with one another and the Father for the sake of the mission. He makes that abundantly clear:

"As you sent me into the world, I have sent them into the world."[16]

Jesus would send his first-century followers into the world with the identical mission and purpose with which he was sent. But what would happen when that original group was gone? What about the generations to follow?

"My prayer is not for *them* alone."[17]

Implication: But it *is* the same prayer.

"I pray also for *those* who will believe in me through their message."[18]

Who's "those"?

Jews. Gentiles. Romans. Samaritans. Women. Slaves. Freedmen. Soldiers. Tax collectors. Zealots. The educated and not so educated. The poor, middle class, wealthy, and super wealthy. Brown, Black, Beige, and White. Young and old. Single, married, divorced, remarried. Republicans, Democrats, Independents, and Indecisives.

You. Me. Us.

And what was his request? What was our Lord most concerned about as it relates to you, me, us, and that diverse list of folks mentioned above?

"I pray also for *those* who will believe in me through their message, that *all* of *them* may be *one* . . ."[19]

That's a lot of one. But he wasn't done.

". . . that *all* of *them* may be *one*, Father, *just as* you are in me and I am in you."[20]

One for the win.

One *is* the win.

We are not winning.

We're not winning, as Jesus defined winning, because we've decided that something else is more important than oneness. As a result, to leverage Paul's words, we are biting, devouring, and destroying one another.[21] We're running the wrong race. We're striving for the wrong prize. We are more concerned about the loss of religious liberty than our loss of unity. We're more concerned about who's in the White House than we are about the division in the church. We're more concerned about everything there is to be concerned about than we are the one thing Jesus was most concerned about.

When *one* is my win, I lose my right to size you up and write you off. Regardless of who you voted for. When *one* becomes your win, you lose your right to write me off as well. We lose our right to write one another off, because neither the Father nor the Son wrote us off. Instead, they redeemed us and invited us to join . . . *them*. And when we join them, their agenda becomes our agenda. There's less that divides us. More that unifies us. Because . . .

It won't be about us.

We can't continue to allow it to be about us—we can't continue to allow politics to divide us—because there is too much at stake.

How much is at stake? Jesus tells us. Please don't rush by this:

"May *they* also be in us *so that* . . ."[22]

"So that" indicates a purpose clause. The purpose of our unity is

". . . so that the *world* may believe that *you* have sent *me*."[23]

Unity is not a "nice to have." Unity is mission critical.

We cannot accomplish the will of God without unity because unity *is* the will of God. God's will for you is that you become one in purpose with me. God's will for me is that I would endeavor not to allow anything to divide me from you. The more unalike we are, the better. The more reason we have to dislike one another, the brighter. The legitimate and not-so-legitimate reasons you have to dislike me are opportunities. The legitimate and not-so-legitimate reasons I have to avoid and criticize you are opportunities as well.

We shouldn't miss 'em.

We should capitalize on 'em.

Unity is mission critical because unity authenticates our message. It makes us credible and convincing. Disunity makes us, well, it makes us like everybody else. Public shaming, theological elitism, heresy hunting, name-calling—those confirm the suspicions of those looking for reasons to size us up and write us off as posers, users, and hypocrites. That behavior undermines our influence, silences our voices, and causes outsiders to wonder why we insist on referring to our message as *good news*.

The enemy of the church is not the other political party.

The enemy of the church is division.

The way forward is simple. Not easy. Simple. We must choose unity over party. We must choose one another. Our commitment to and love for one another must publicly supplant our commitment to political brands and talking points. And when our party of choice requires a choice that conflicts with Jesus's new-covenant, one-another brand of love . . .

Well, that's when we discover who and whose we truly are.

One is the win.

One is the win because one positions us to win.

Not elections.

People.

Your party will win or lose based on voter turnout on a given Tuesday in November.

The church will win or lose—our communities will win or lose—based on our response to Jesus's new-covenant command and our refusal to let anything or anyone divide us.

Chuck Mingo, a pastor and the founder of Living Undivided, says it well: "We can't preach a united gospel as a divided church."[24]

With so much at stake, why would we allow ourselves to be divided by the promises of lesser kings? Why would we allow a political view to divide us from the living, breathing "you" across the street or across the aisle? The you beside you. The you next door to you. Why would we not fight for, struggle for, and sacrifice for the *unity* our King prayed for?

Jesus prayed for oneness because he believed it was possible. He prayed for oneness because it's essential. It doesn't come naturally. We will have to fight for it. Forgive for it. Serve for it. Lose for it. But remember, it was Christianity—not the Republican Party or the Democratic Party—that shaped Western civilization. It was the teaching of Jesus—not our political parties—that laid the groundwork for our modern sense of justice, fairness, and dignity of the individual.

Am I being naive?

No.

I'll tell you what's naive.

A rabbi from nowhere standing in the middle of pretty much nowhere, baking in the hot Syrian sun with twelve young men, making this audacious promise:

"I will build my church, and the gates of Hades will not overcome it."[25]

That's naive. But he *did*. And it *didn't*. And we are *part* of it.

I'm not naive. I'm hopeful.

So one last time: What do you pray for?

Would you be willing to pray for what Jesus prayed for? Would you add the following to your prayer routine: "Heavenly Father, make us *one* and begin with *me*."

Christians will always disagree politically. But it's possible to disagree politically without it disrupting our *unity*.

Jesus thought so.

He prayed so.

Let's do so.

CHAPTER SEVEN

THE SUPPER OF GOD

I n light of the previous two chapters, or even a casual reading of the Gospels, one thing should be abundantly clear. There is no room in the Jesus movement for cruelty, violence, or the threat of violence. We are to be winsome so that we might win some. As *followers* of Jesus, we should be like Jesus. He didn't size people up and write 'em off. We shouldn't either.

With that in mind, I would like to invite Christian leaders everywhere to break with a tradition many of us inherited from previous generations of Christians. A tradition that was grafted *into* our faith from *outside* our faith. A tradition leveraged before the Reformation, that was elevated to literally breathtaking heights during the Reformation. A tradition that has diluted and distracted Christianity for centuries.

What exactly am I talking about?

The age-old tradition—and bad habit—of importing warfare language and conflict imagery into a faith whose central figure surrendered his life rather than defending it and who invited his followers to follow suit.

Fortunately, the varying streams of our faith are no longer *literally* at war with one another as was the case in the sixteenth and seventeenth centuries. But the language of warfare and conquest continues to permeate our vocabulary, slip into our sermons, and shape our posture toward disturbing cultural trends.

So let's be the generation of Jesus followers that buries this longstanding tradition. A tradition that undermines our credibility. Worse, a tradition that stands in stark contrast with the message, posture, and approach of our Savior.

Jesus was not at war with anyone.

The church is his body.

So it stands to reason that the church is not at war with anyone.

As Jesus followers, we shouldn't be or pretend to be at war with anyone either. We have no business borrowing, importing, or continuing to use language or metaphors that leave an impression to the contrary. The apostle Paul made this point. The same apostle Paul whose religious liberty and life were literally threatened every day following his decision to follow Jesus. He wrote,

Our struggle is *not* against flesh and blood.[1]

Paul was convinced our actual struggle isn't against other people but against schemes of the devil.[2] Apparently, one of the devil's favorite schemes is to confuse us as to whom our struggle is truly against. It's certainly an effective scheme. A kingdom divided against itself ruins itself.[3]

To be clear: There are plenty of individuals and organizations who view the church as an enemy. Lots of folks would be elated (for a minute) if organized religion ceased to be. They don't like evangelical Christianity in particular.

But if Jesus was correct—and I believe he was—if someone considers you their enemy, you're not required to return the favor. Someone can go to war with you while you refuse to go to war with them.

Got teenagers?

Point made.

Granted, refusing to go to war with an individual or organization that declares war on you is a bit un-American. Actually, it's unnatural. It's unnatural to maintain a peaceful posture in the face of hostility. But it *can* be done. And if we are truly Jesus followers, it *must* be done. Or we're not following. We're just believing. Maintaining a peaceful posture in the face of hostility is a foundational tenet of the kingdom Jesus introduced to the world. It's not an add-on. It's a demarcation, something that sets us apart.

It's required.

Loving our enemies isn't something Jesus *suggested*. It's something he *commanded*.

Jesus commanded us not to go to war with individuals or organizations that consider us the enemy. We are not to repay evil with evil. Or violence with violence.

You may be *their* enemy. But they are not yours.

We may be their enemy. But they are not ours.

Because we are not at war.

With that in mind, here's yet another career-ending suggestion.

NO MORE IMPORTS

Let's discontinue the centuries-old tradition of importing Old Testament military imagery, narratives, and metaphors into our new-covenant preaching, teaching, and application.

They don't belong there.

The conquer and conquest narratives depicted in the Old Testament stand in sharp contrast to the tone and posture of Jesus. Those important narratives are the backstory to the main story. Likewise, we have no business reaching forward into the book of Revelation to import the military imagery associated with our returning, conquering, enemy-slaughtering king.

I'm not being irreverent.

I take the author of Revelation at his word. Don't you?

Both Old Testament and end-times warfare imagery and language are incompatible with the new-covenant mandate of Jesus. A mandate given directly to us. A mandate to love, make disciples, and lay down our lives in the process if necessary.

The Gospels and Epistles are unmistakably clear. We are not in it to win anything. Jesus already won it. Jesus will win it again. In the meantime, we are to love one another and the people around us in such a way that we are *winsome* whether we win anything or not.

Walk to Emmaus? That's fine.

Jericho march?

Not so fine.

We are not Israel. You are not Joshua. We're pro-life, remember? The original Jericho march left babies and children buried under rubble. Instead, we are to love, serve, forgive, and submit to one another. We are to carry one another's burdens. And, in the apostle Paul's words, we are to

> . . . be wise in the way you act toward outsiders; make the most of every opportunity.[4]

You are to

> . . . let your conversation be always full of grace, seasoned with salt, so that you may know how to answer everyone.[5]

When our conversation is *full* of salt and merely *seasoned* with grace, we're not doing it right.

Refusing to import Old Testament imagery that conflicts with our new-covenant mandate isn't just about theological correctness. It's about the Great Commission. It's about evangelism. It's about the *ekklesia* of Jesus functioning as seasoned salt and unfiltered light. It's about ensuring that the life-changing *new* that Jesus unleashed in the world doesn't get retrofitted with something old or something reserved for the future. Retro is fine for your middle school daughter's bedroom. Cinematic depictions of the final apocalypse are great for entertainment. Neither is fine for the church.

To paraphrase James, the brother of Jesus, our job is to not make it unnecessarily difficult for those who are turning to God.[6] To paraphrase the apostle Paul, this is about winning some and saving some.[7] Conquer and conflict language slows us down, divides us up, and confuses those standing on the outside peering in. Centuries of importing from the old and borrowing from the future to supplement and illustrate our new-covenant faith has resulted in a version of faith infested with shadows from the past. Paul thought so anyway. Referring to old-covenant leftovers, he wrote,

> These are a *shadow* of the things that were to come; the reality, however, is found in Christ.[8]

You can discern some things about an object by the shadow it casts. But not everything. The Sinai covenant and many of the Old Testament narratives served as shadows. But now the reality has come. You want to know what God is like? You want to know who God likes? You want to know what God acts like? Philip did.

> "Lord, show us the Father and that will be enough for us."[9]

Remember Jesus's response? Instead of referring Philip to the Scriptures, he referred Philip to himself!

Who would do that?

> Jesus answered: "Don't you know me, Philip, even after I have been among you such a long time? Anyone who has seen me has seen the Father."[10]

Q: Who needs shadows when the reality has come?

A: People who prefer shadows.

Old-covenant imports explain why some religious leaders feel it's their responsibility to rail against the evils in society like an Old Testament prophet. Paul told Christians in Corinth that the behavior of unbelievers was none of their business.[11] He assured them that God would judge those outside the faith.

As mentioned earlier, we are not at war with the culture. Culture-war Christianity is not simply a waste of time, it is diametrically opposed to the teaching of Paul and the example of Jesus. As it relates to the influence of the church, our nation's challenges do not stem from the church's inability to convince unbelievers to behave like believers. Our challenges stem from the church's inability to inspire believers to behave like believers.

Bad church experiences are almost always related to somebody taking a stand that leaves them standing on someone. Most bad church experiences are the result of somebody prioritizing a *view* over a *you*—something Jesus never did and instructed us not to do either. In my experience, the justifications Christians use to mistreat people are often rooted in old-covenant practices, narratives, and values.

SOMETHING BORROWED, SOMETHING NEW

To be clear: I'm not suggesting that the covenant God made with Israel at Mount Sinai was flawed. Just the opposite. When understood in its ancient context, it was brilliant! The civil and religious law detailed in God's arrangement with ancient Israel was superior in every way to the civil and religious law of the surrounding nations. The Torah provided protections for the most vulnerable. This was nothing short of revolutionary in its original context. Women, servants, foreigners, and children all fared better under Hebrew law than did their counterparts in surrounding regions.

But as brilliant and ahead of its time as it was, it was God's covenant or contract with ancient Israel. Not you. Not me. Not only was the Sinai covenant, as it is sometimes referred to, created for the benefit of a specific group of people, it was created for a specific time frame as well. God's Sinai covenant with Israel was temporary. Important, strategic, divinely ordained, but temporary. It was a means to an end. In Christ, it came to an end.

God's covenant with Israel was a necessary step between his promise to Abraham and the fulfillment of that promise through Christ. From a nation of redeemed slaves God brought forth the Redeemer of the world.

As his followers, we have no business retrofitting his current kingdom values, posture, language, and approach to persuasion with the values, posture, and language he came to replace. When we attempt to shore up our Christianity with Old Testament win-lose, conquer-and-vanquish language, we do just that. Beginning with Abraham. God went to work fashioning a nation from dirt. That required a specific set of tools. If the God of the Hebrews was going to establish a nation for himself, he would have to wade into the fray and play by the rules of the day.

Which is exactly what he did.

God played by the rules of the kingdoms of this world to usher in a kingdom not of this world through a covenant that stands as an invitation to everyone in the world. It's what makes the story of the exodus epic. YHWH spoke and acted in a way Pharaoh could understand and used the only things an Egyptian pharaoh would understand—power and violence. We don't need to be embarrassed by that. We don't need to sanitize and spiritualize it. We certainly don't need to harmonize it with the Sermon on the Mount. It is what it is.

Attempts to civilize the terms, conditions, and outcomes of the old covenant and its associated narratives undermine the credibility of the text and the credibility of the church. Worse, doing so diminishes the extent to which God went to redeem and rescue the world from sin.

The Old Testament is a saga of an ancient people

struggling to survive in a world where food was scarce, enemies were real, and death was just a minor infection away. In spite of that, they clung to YHWH, and he in turn clung to his nation, careful not to override their freedom with his presence. It's gritty. Bloody. Tragic. Real. It's ancient history with a divine purpose.

But then . . .

When the time was right, when God had everything just the way he wanted it, he sent a baby, born of a woman, born under the old covenant with all its violent, bloody history. The Word became flesh and dwelled among us. He lived among us as one of us. But unlike us,

> he made himself nothing
>> by taking the very nature of a servant . . .

And in the end . . .

>> he humbled himself
>> by becoming obedient to death—
>>> even death on a cross![12]

Surrender? Death? How passive! Defeatist! What happened to an eye for an eye? Where's the shepherd boy and his sling? Where's Joshua and his slingers? Where are the angel armies?

The angel armies were there.

They were standing by. Standing down. Aghast at what they beheld.

God waded into our story to initiate the story of our redemption. And he saw it played out to the bitter, bloody, "Crucify him, crucify him!" end.

By old-covenant, kingdoms-of-this-world standards, Jesus lost.

By new-covenant, kingdom-of-God standards, he won.

We do others and ourselves a great disservice when we retrofit the cultural values, behaviors, and narratives of the Old Testament to make them compatible with the new. First-century Jewish Jesus followers felt no compulsion to tidy up and remove the sharp edges from the Old Testament. It wasn't their problem. In fact, it *wasn't* a problem.

Something new had come.

Let's not make it *old* again.

When we import warfare imagery from the Old Testament into our new-covenant way of life, we do just that. When we reach back, we step back. When we reach back, we lose our distinctive. When we accept the weapons of coercion offered us by the kingdoms of this world, we look just like 'em because we start behaving, responding, sounding, and tweeting like 'em.

Leveraging old-covenant conquest and warfare imagery distorts the way of Jesus.

On the night of his arrest, Jesus inaugurated something new. The *new* Jesus unleashed made the faith of first-century believers formidable. Their apologetic was irrefutable.

Their courage, unquestionable. The results were remarkable. Reaching back into old-covenant warfare narratives or ahead into *end-time* imagery undermines the message of Jesus for *our time* and conflicts with the posture and tone he modeled and commanded us to emulate.

If you want to fight for your rights as an American citizen, have at it. I'll join you.

But let's not invite Jesus to the fight.

It's not his fight.

BEEN THERE

So, you ask, where is all this passion coming from? Well, I've been there, done that, and I'm done with that. Actually, I never actually participated in that. Because I saw where that leads. You've seen where it leads as well. It leads to a generation that grew up in church and is now in the process of deconstructing their faith.

I grew up with a version of Christianity that sang about the love of Jesus but adopted a posture that felt a bit Old Testament-ish. It was very we-they. We were God's people, *they* weren't. We were blessable. They weren't. If any of *they* chose to put their faith in Jesus and join us, great! But until then, *they* were *they* and *we* were *we*.

And *they* were out to get us.

We were at war.

They were out to corrupt our children. Secularize our schools. Undermine our religious freedom. They wanted to lure us away from our faith. Sermons were filled with references to them, they, the ungodly, the blind, the deceived, the immoral, and the wicked. And while we paid lip service to Paul's insistence that our struggle was *not* against flesh and blood, we preached, prayed, and behaved as if it most certainly was.

That mindset made it easy to adopt, import, recontextualize, and apply all manner of Old Testament conflict and conquest narratives—narratives we sanitized and romanticized in the telling so as not to offend modern sensibilities. Once the gore was gone, those images were easy to incorporate. We were the Israelites, they were the Canaanites, Amalekites, and Egyptians. We were Joshua, they were Jericho. We were David, they were Goliath. We were the persecuted remnant, but we would win in the end! The book of Revelation guaranteed it.

We loved Revelation.

Sermon on the Mount?

Not so much.

Far too impractical. Nobody could actually live that way, we said. So we convinced ourselves Jesus was talking to someone else. Perhaps people in the age to come. After the enemies of God were vanquished and their entrails consumed by birds of prey.

Did I mention we loved Revelation?

The book of Revelation confirmed the legitimacy of our wartime posture. There was, in fact, going to be a war. Jesus was going to initiate it! He was coming back . . .

but not in passive, turn-the-other-cheek, shepherd-martyr mode.

Hell no.

Actually, hell yes.

He was coming back with a sword in his mouth, an iron scepter in his hand, fire in his eyes, and the wrath of God on his breath.

> I saw heaven standing open and there before me was
> a white horse, whose rider is called Faithful and True.
> With justice he judges and *wages war*.[13]

General Jesus.

> His eyes are like blazing fire, and on his head are
> many crowns. He has a name written on him that
> no one knows but he himself. He is dressed in a robe
> dipped in blood, and his name is the Word of God.[14]

Jesus is wearing a robe stained with someone else's blood. Ancient warriors who survived a battle always emerged covered in the blood of their enemies. There was little distance killing in ancient warfare. You knew what your enemy had for breakfast. If you survived, your garment was stained with it.

> The armies of heaven were following him, riding on
> white horses and dressed in fine linen, white and

clean. Coming out of his mouth is a sharp sword with which to strike down the nations. "He will rule them with an iron scepter."[15]

A sword and a scepter. He will not be messing around.

He treads the winepress of the fury of the wrath of God Almighty. On his robe and on his thigh, he has this name written:

KING OF KINGS AND LORD OF LORDS.[16]

And the enemies of Jesus?

I saw an angel standing in the sun, who cried in a loud voice to all the birds flying in midair, "Come, gather together for *the great supper of God*."[17]

And what's on the menu for "the great supper of God"?

So that you may eat the flesh of kings, generals, and the mighty, of horses and their riders, and the *flesh of all people*, free and slave, great and small.[18]

This is where the sanitizing generally begins. But to sanitize this text is to miss the picture the author of Revelation intends to present. "The great supper of God" is a banquet for the birds. The author is clear: the birds will feast on the flesh of humans. Not angels or demons. People. All kinds of people.

When birds of prey descended on an ancient battlefield, they did not distinguish between the wounded and the dead. They preferred those still in the process of bleeding out. It's why birds of prey descended quickly. Birds began with the soft tissue. The eyes. Then the lips and tongue. Then the groin area. By the time the first course comes to an end, jackals and hyenas have caught the scent of the stench and make their way to the smorgasbord of human gore.

This is "the great supper of God."

I'm not being irreverent.

I'm not being overly literal.

This is the scene the first-century author of Revelation wants his first-century audience to picture. He did not include the detail I added because his first-century audience knew the horror of the aftermath of hand-to-hand warfare.

Think of it this way: if I told you I had my teeth cleaned last week, I wouldn't need to explain the process. You've been there and done that. All the details are etched in your memory. "Teeth cleaning" is all the description you need. So it was with the aftermath of combat in ancient times. Nobody needed the details. It was horror beyond our modern imaginations. According to the author of Revelation, this particular horror will be initiated by our Savior.

I saw the beast and the kings of the earth and their armies gathered together to wage war against the rider on the horse and his army. But the beast was captured, and with it the false prophet who had performed the signs on its behalf. With these signs he had deluded those who had received the mark of the beast and worshiped its image. The two of them were thrown *alive* into the fiery lake of burning sulfur. The rest were killed with the sword coming out of the mouth of the rider on the horse, and all the *birds gorged themselves* on their flesh.[19]

More gorging birds.

This is how it ends. Christians win!

But . . .

And this is why I catapulted our discussion to the end of days. But who initiates and wages this war against the enemies of God? Christians? The church?

No.

According to the author, this is Jesus's war.

LOOKING FORWARD

As disturbing as all that sounds, I've never met a Christian who was all that disturbed by it. In the churches I grew up in, folks seemed to relish the thought of a final, bloody, violent victory over God's enemies. Enemies who never once threatened violence against them. Enemies who didn't consider themselves our enemies because they didn't con-sider us at all. They weren't against us. They weren't trying to corrupt us.

For the most part they ignored us.

We were at war with an enemy who wasn't aware there *was* a war. But that didn't matter. What mattered was that in the end we would win. And our enemies, who didn't know there was a war, would suffer mightily. Because they deserved it. After all, they had . . . well, in the end they would get what they deserved, and we would get what we . . . what we didn't deserve. They would be eaten by birds and we would participate in the marriage supper of the Lamb.

Anyway.

It didn't all make sense, but that didn't matter. What mattered is that in the end we would win. We just needed to hunker down, remain unstained by the world, and pray for the great supper of God! The second coming of Christ. To encourage and inspire us, our denomination had an anthem to support our war footing. It was printed in our hymnals.

> Onward, Christian soldiers,
> marching as to war,
> With the cross of Jesus
> going on before!
> Christ, the royal Master,
> leads against the foe;
> Forward into battle,
> see his banner go!

At the sign of triumph
Satan's host doth flee;
On, then, Christian soldiers,
on to victory!

We were in it to win it.

And who could blame us? The Bible begins with warfare between God's people and their enemies, and it ends with more of the same. There are winners and there are losers. In the end, Christians win.

NOT THE FIRST

We aren't the first generation of Christians to smuggle warfare language and imagery into our new-covenant faith. Constantine painted the Chi-Rho—a monogram of the first two letters of Christ's name in Greek—on the shields of his soldiers. In ancient warfare, a shield was a weapon. The abbreviated name of Christ would be the last thing many in Maxentius's infantry would see before their faces were mangled by the bronze-rimmed shields of Constantine's disciplined infantry.

Seven hundred years later, Pope Urban II promised the remission of all sin for anyone participating in a military campaign to liberate the Holy Land from Muslim infidels.

Don't rush by that.

The pope, successor to Saint Peter, initiated a *military* campaign. Not to liberate people from sin. To liberate real estate from sinners. There are several versions of his recruitment speech. Here's an interesting, if not disputed, passage: "All who die by the way, whether by land or by sea, or in battle against the pagans, shall have immediate remission of sins. This I grant them through the power of God with which I am invested."[20]

Forgiveness in exchange for military service. Not too dissimilar from promises made by religious extremists in our generation. God wanted his land back! He wanted his city back! And it was his will that anyone who resisted be put to the sword. So said Christ's vicar.

Urban's speeches unleashed unspeakable violence against all God's "enemies." Knights throughout Europe sewed crosses on their tunics and went to war in Jesus's name. Crusaders took control of Jerusalem in July 1099. They massacred tens of thousands of Muslims and anyone mistaken for a Muslim. Survivors were sold as slaves.

Modern historians argue that the Crusades were perhaps justified in light of their geopolitical context. But no one attempts to justify the church's use of the Bible to sanction the slaughter that occurred. Church leaders weaponized Christianity by offering a get-out-of-hell-free card. Church officials leveraged Old Testament texts to justify violence while promising a New Testament heaven for those who participated.

Throughout the disturbing era of the Crusades, Jews were murdered by the thousands and their property confiscated. Why? Jews were responsible for crucifying Jesus.

They were enemies of God. The Old Testament was clear. Enemies of God *must* be punished. The book of Revelation was clear. God's enemies *will* be punished.

God willed it!

God will will it again!

Apparently, God only temporarily willed it. Eighty-eight years later, in 1187, Saladin, a Sunni Muslim Kurd, led Muslim forces to retake the city of Jerusalem. For the next forty years, European Crusaders attempted and failed to retake the city.

Atrocities carried out in the name of Christ in subsequent years would be considered terrorism by modern standards. Cruelty was camouflaged with a cross. Hypocrisy draped itself in fine robes. Torture and murder were justified as rites of purification. Violence was justified because, well, Christians were fighting a war. A war against evil. A war against heresy. A war against the enemies of God. And justification for just about anything that needed justifying could be found in the Bible!

But not the entire Bible.

Not the part about Jesus.

Not the parts that describe the post-resurrection activities of his first-century followers.

Not the part written to us, his church.

THAT'S HIS BUSINESS

If Jesus chooses to wage a literal war against his human enemies at a future date, that's up to him.

That's Jesus's business.

It's not your business. It's not my business. It's not the church's business. Jesus may come on a literal white horse or in an F-35C. That's up to him. He may literally smite his enemies with fire and watch them burn. If he wants to appear with a sword in his mouth, that's his business. If he chooses to leave a banquet of human flesh for the birds, that's his business. How and when and if he chooses to accomplish all of that is his business.

If all that is figurative and represents something else entirely, that's his business as well.

What Jesus commanded us to do is our business. We should mind our own business. We should get back to business. We should look for feet to wash, not a war to fight.

Persecuted second- and third-century church leaders would agree. They didn't view their clash with culture as a war. They viewed it in terms of mission. According to historian John Dickson:

> They believed that true power to change the world lay not in politics, the judiciary, or the military but in the message of Christ's resurrection. . . .
>
> This is what made Christians good, even cheerful, losers—the thought that they had *already won*! Their role was simply to remain true to the way of Christ, seeking to transform the world through prayer, service, persuasion and suffering.[21]

Once again, we aren't David fighting Goliath or Israel conquering Canaan. We aren't Joshua marching around the walls of Jericho. We are Jesus followers. We won because he lost. So now we are free to love our enemies and pray for those who persecute us, even if they declare war on us.

When the music stops and the opportunity for choosing ends, Judge Jesus will appear. We will all stand in line and await our turn. In the meantime, we are to do everything in our power to rescue people from impending judgment. We are neither judge nor jury. We are *followers*.

Now, if all this strikes you as passive and permissive, I get it. If you choose to stop reading at this point and continue to opt for a more aggressive, militaristic version of faith, I understand.

So would the gentleman who wrote almost half of the New Testament.

Saul of Tarsus was a warrior. God's warrior. He was in it to win it. Then he met Jesus.

Then he wrote a series of letters that shaped Western civilization.

So perhaps you should stick around for one more chapter.

CHAPTER EIGHT

INQUISITOR IN CHIEF

L uke, the author of the third gospel, holds the distinction of introducing us to the individual responsible for almost half the words in the New Testament: Saul of Tarsus. Luke's introduction is less than flattering. It's so unflattering no one would have suspected the trajectory and impact of Saul's life. Luke introduces us to Saul outside the walls of Jerusalem at a stoning. But not just any stoning. The victim, Stephen, would eventually be celebrated and remembered as the first Christian martyr.

His crime?

There wasn't one.

But the cult he represented had gained unexpected and unexplainable momentum and needed to be crushed. So "witnesses" were procured and furnished with scripts—scripts accusing Stephen of repeating threats against the temple and the Torah that were originally articulated by Jesus of Nazareth, who hadn't been seen in several months. But that didn't matter. What mattered was Stephen was a spokesperson for a foul Nazarene sect that insisted Jesus was divine. So Stephen had to go. And go he did.

Peacefully.

"Lord," he prayed, "do not hold this sin against them."[1]

How was it that this Jewish knockoff cult had gained so much traction when its adherents all gave up without a fight? They didn't go down swinging.

They went down praying.

It was baffling. Nevertheless, this movement needed to be checked before the contagion spread any further. And young Saul of Tarsus heartily agreed. So says Luke.

But . . .

It's important to remember that Luke, who also authored Acts, eventually accompanied Saul on his missionary journeys around the Mediterranean basin. They became friends. So the detail Luke includes in his account of Stephen's stoning isn't conjecture. Luke didn't have to imagine what Saul was thinking. He had source material. And it cast the most famous Christian in history in an extraordinarily negative light. Luke tells us:

Saul *approved* of their *killing* him.[2]

If my graphic description of the supper of God in the last chapter seemed unwarranted, it wasn't. What's unwarranted is attempting to sanitize the brutality that characterized the ancient world. Similarly, it would be particularly unwarranted to sanitize Saul's story because of the lesson embedded in it—a lesson that rarely gets the attention it deserves.

Luke didn't elaborate on the violence associated with Stephen's stoning for the same reason the author of Revelation didn't go into detail about the aftermath of battle. Luke doesn't elaborate on the horror of Stephen's stoning for the same reason he didn't go into detail regarding Jesus's crucifixion. None of the gospel writers did. Here's Luke's description of the event that changed the world:

> When they came to the place called the Skull, they crucified him there.[3]

That's it.

No details.

None were needed. Most of Luke's first-century readers had seen a crucifixion or the aftermath of one or knew someone who could describe one if they were interested. We've never witnessed crucifixion or stoning. We've only imagined such things. Mostly incorrectly.

Stoning was mob action. It was terrifying for the victim. In most instances, it was carried out by a pack of enraged, self-deputized locals convinced they were carrying out justice. In Stephen's case, his executioners were confident they acted with God's stamp of approval. After all, the high priest himself signed off on Stephen's guilt. Stephen was a blasphemer. Blasphemers were to be put to death.

God willed it.

In first-century Judea, there was no official protocol for

stoning. The only stipulations were that it had to take place outside the city walls and that the victim's accusers cast the first stones as evidence that their testimony was true.

Luke's account of Stephen's stoning gives the impression of a crowd so worked up they were barely outside the city walls before hostilities commenced. Victims of stoning were often unconscious rather than dead at the end of the ordeal. To ensure the process ended as intended, a large stone, often carried by more than one individual, was dropped directly on the victim's chest or head.

This is what Saul of Tarsus, the author of *the* iconic love poem read at weddings every weekend, observed, endorsed, and celebrated.

And that was only the beginning.

Stephen's uncontested public execution opened a floodgate. It was open season on followers of the Way. And we all know who led the way to exterminate the Way.

> On that day a great persecution broke out against the church in Jerusalem, and all except the apostles were scattered throughout Judea and Samaria. Godly men buried Stephen and mourned deeply for him.[4]

Godly men mourned. But the mourning was just beginning.

> Saul began to *destroy* the church. Going from house to house, he dragged off both men and women and put them in prison.[5]

Read that again. But this time picture your family. Your wife. Your children.

> Going from house to house, he *dragged* off both men *and* women and put them in prison.[6]

Later, in his own words,

> I persecuted the followers of this Way to their *death*, arresting both men and women and throwing them into prison.[7]

There were no actual *prisons* in the first century. The Greek term translated *prison* in our English Bible refers to any place a prisoner was held—often a hole in the ground. Not a concrete-lined hole with drainage. Just a hole in the ground. Dark, damp, bug-infested, human-feces-saturated. No drainage. No meal plan. When they ran out of holes, they doubled up.

Picture it. Imagine it. You. Your children. Your spouse.

Just as it's important not to rush by the violence associated with Paul's preconversion activities, it's equally important not to rush by his justification for his seemingly over-the-top zeal. Preachers and teachers are quick to point out his sincerity. He believed he was doing God's bidding by destroying the church. That's true. But to stop there is to miss the broader point, the point Paul goes out of his way to make.

Paul's justification for violence was hitched to something

far more consequential than personal religious zeal. He says so himself. He wasn't merely defending his religion.

He was fulfilling the Torah. Not his interpretation of the Torah but the standard interpretation.

I'll let him explain:

> I studied under Gamaliel and was *thoroughly trained* in the law of our ancestors. I was just as zealous for God as any of you are today.[8]

Paul studied under the best of the best. He was *thoroughly trained*. In his letter to Christians in Philippi, he includes a bit of biographical information along with some employment history:

> Circumcised on the eighth day, of the people of Israel, of the tribe of Benjamin, a Hebrew of Hebrews; in regard to the law, a Pharisee; as for zeal, persecuting the church; as for righteousness based on the law, *faultless*.[9]

Faultless.

Quite a claim! To Christians living in the Roman province of Galatia, he wrote:

> You have heard of my previous way of life in Judaism, how intensely I persecuted the church of God and tried to destroy it. I was advancing in Judaism beyond

many of my own age among my people and was extremely *zealous* for the *traditions* of my fathers.[10]

Paul's justification for violence against members of the Way came directly from his educated interpretation of his sacred texts. His actions were rooted in and informed by his reading of the first five books of your Old Testament. He wasn't making stuff up. He was keeping up. He was acting in accordance with the law of Moses. God's covenant with Israel mandated Paul's behavior. He wasn't trying for extra credit. He was merely satisfying the demands of the law.

The law demanded violent retribution against any Hebrew who worshiped anyone or anything other than YHWH, even family members:

If your very own brother, or your son or daughter, or the wife you love, or your closest friend secretly entices you, saying, "Let us go and worship other gods" . . . do not yield to them or listen to them. Show them no pity. Do not spare them or shield them. You must certainly put them to death. Your hand must be the first in putting them to death, and then the hands of all the people. Stone them to death, because they tried to turn you away from the LORD your God, who brought you out of Egypt, out of the land of slavery.[11]

Pretty clear.
Equally clear.

Followers of the Way worshiped Jesus. They considered him divine. The Son of Man. This was blasphemy of the first order. They had to go.

Paul wasn't the only one who felt empowered to leverage violence against apostate Jews. He wasn't alone in finding justification for violence in the Torah. His superiors concurred. His boss back in Jerusalem deputized him to carry out violence against the blasphemers. He gave Paul letters to take to the folks overseeing the synagogue in Damascus, requesting names and numbers of anyone suspected of being associated with the Way. Once Paul tracked 'em down, he was to cart them back to Jerusalem to stand trial. If unwilling to recant, they too would possibly be dragged outside the city walls and stoned.

Paul's deputizing boss was none other than the high priest. Imagine that. The high priest, a man intimately acquainted with the sacred texts, had no qualms about commissioning Paul to arrest and, if need be, exterminate followers of the Way.

And Paul wasn't acting alone. Several weeks after his conversion in Damascus, while he was still *in* Damascus, local Torah followers conspired to . . . wait for it . . . *kill him.*

After many days had gone by, there was a conspiracy among the Jews to kill him, but Saul learned of their plan. Day and night they kept close watch on the city gates in order to kill him.[12]

Debating with Saul got them nowhere. But instead of agreeing to disagree, they decided to *murder* him! Not arrest and cart him back to Jerusalem to stand trial. Lynch him. And they felt completely justified in doing so. Back in Jerusalem they would be considered heroes.

Fortunately for the world, Saul's friends helped him escape. They sent him on his way to Jerusalem, where he received a less-than-warm welcome. He was so feared by believers that even after word of his conversion circulated, Jesus followers in Damascus and Jerusalem were terrified to go near him. Of course they were. He had led the inquisition. He was the persecutor in chief. He had blood on his hands—the blood of their friends and family members. Luke describes it this way:

> When he came to Jerusalem, he tried to join the disciples, but they were all afraid of him, not believing that he really was a disciple.[13]

If you've read the book of Acts, you know Saul, known by most as Paul, spent his entire ministry looking over his shoulder. He was hated and hunted. During a return visit to Jerusalem years later, he had to be rescued from temple officials by a Roman officer. After debating with Paul and with one another, the temple officials became so violent that the attending centurion ordered his men to take Paul to their barracks to keep him from being "torn to pieces."[14]

Torn to pieces.

Here's what happened next:

> The next morning some Jews formed a conspiracy
> and bound themselves with an oath not to eat or
> drink until they had killed Paul. More than forty
> men were involved in this plot.[15]

And whose assistance did they retain?

> They went to the chief priests and the elders and said,
> "We have taken a solemn oath not to eat anything
> until we have killed Paul. Now then, you and the
> Sanhedrin petition the commander to bring him
> before you on the pretext of wanting more accurate
> information about his case. We are ready to kill him
> before he gets here."[16]

Once again, Paul cheated death—this time with the
help of his nephew and his new BFF, the Roman centurion.

WAR NO MORE

Before his conversion, Paul was a living example of what the
old covenant looked like and behaved like. When operating
under the authority of the old covenant, he was free to
track down, arrest, torture, and execute apostate Jews.
According to his understanding of the Hebrew Scriptures,

his unbridled cruelty was God's will. He was doing God's work. Paul, who prided himself on being the most law-abiding Pharisee in the Middle East, believed he was acting on God's behalf when he assumed the role of inquisitor and executioner. When we read or hear about the unimaginable atrocities carried out in the name of Christianity in the decades and centuries that followed, we wonder how such things could be justified. Paul knew.

He'd been there and done that.

But once he met Jesus, he was done with that. All of that. Why?

Read his letters.

The old covenant *demanded* it!

The new covenant *forbade* it!

Paul found nothing in the teaching of Jesus or his apostles to justify violent opposition against those who violently opposed the Way.

Don't rush by that.

This is a lesson from Paul's life that our habit of mixing and blending covenants enables us to overlook. When Paul became a Jesus follower, he could find nothing in the teaching of Jesus or his apostles to justify violent opposition to those who would violently oppose him and the movement he'd become a part of. He found the very opposite. As he would write years later:

If, while we were God's *enemies*, we were *reconciled* to him through the death of his Son, how much more, having been reconciled, shall we be saved through his life![17]

King Jesus died for his enemies and thus paved the way for his enemies to be rescued, restored, and reconciled to their King. If his Savior refused to go to war with evil men, Paul knew he lost his right to do so as well. His encounter with Jesus signaled an end to all things violent, destructive, and coercive. He laid aside the sanctioned techniques of terror and persuasion. Weaponizing first-century Judaism was easy.

Weaponizing Christianity was impossible.

Violence and the threat of violence were incompatible with, at odds with, and counterproductive to the kingdom and covenant Jesus established. So Paul laid all of that down—and never picked it up again. Others would violently oppose him for the rest of his life. But he refused to return the favor. He refused to resort to violence. His religious liberty wasn't threatened. His tax-exempt status wasn't threatened.

His *life* was threatened.

But like his Savior, he refused to threaten back.

BOTH SIDES OF BOTH COVENANTS

Unlike you, unlike me, Paul lived under and fully embraced the stipulations in God's covenant with ancient Israel. Paul knew from experience that the old and new covenants were incompatible. Mixing and matching them, as many Christians still attempt to do, wasn't something he approved of. To the contrary, he insisted that any attempt to blend old and new resulted in a perversion of Christianity.

A version that readily employs the tools and tactics of the kingdoms of this world. A version where warfare terminology feels right and the Sermon on the Mount sounds weak. A version where cruelty masquerades as taking a stand. Where gossip and slander are justified as heresy hunting. It's the version of Christianity easily deconstructed and abandoned by *ex-vangelicals* today.

After Paul's initial encounter with Jesus, his worldview changed. And not just his understanding of justification and salvation but his entire worldview. He had taken the old covenant to its logical extreme, both in his personal devotion to it, as well as in his no-holds-barred defense of it.

Yet while Paul consistently acknowledged the incomparability of the old and new covenants, he never—as in never ever—questioned the divine origin of the Hebrew Scriptures. And he never felt compelled to sanitize them. They were what they were because of *when* they were written and *for whom* they were written. They were a divinely inspired means to a divinely ordained end, which positioned Messiah Jesus as both a beginning and an end.

The end of something old.

The beginning of something new.

Paul knew how easily the legalism, hypocrisy, self-righteousness, and exclusivity of first-century Judaism could seep into and erode the beauty, simplicity, and appeal of the good news Jesus introduced. Paul's graphic imagery in Galatians reveals the depth of his zeal to maintain the purity and exclusivity of the new covenant. When word reached him that evangelists for the blended covenant version of faith were misleading gentile believers in Galatia, he responded immediately and directly.

> I am astonished that you are so quickly deserting the one who called you to live in the grace of Christ and are turning to a different gospel—which is really no gospel at all. Evidently some people are throwing you into confusion and are trying to pervert the gospel of Christ.[18]

Paul calls the blended covenant model a "perversion."

> But even if we or an angel from heaven should preach a gospel other than the one we preached to you, let them be under God's curse![19]

A curse? Paul calls down a curse on the missionaries preaching mix-and-match. For good measure, he repeats himself.

> As we have already said, so now I say again: If anybody is preaching to you a gospel other than what you accepted, let them be under God's curse![20]

That's harsh. But we salvation-by-faith-alone types can't help but cheer him on. Right? After all, he's defending the gospel. Grace alone. Faith alone. Christ alone. But Paul was doing more than that. We miss the "more than that" part because of how we've heard these passages taught. This is what we hear: If anyone tries to convince you that salvation comes through the works of the law rather than grace, let them be under God's curse!

Not only is that not what he said, but that's not what he meant. The issue Paul was responding to in the Galatian churches was not limited to how one gains salvation. The issue was the relevance of the *entire* Mosaic covenant. The Judaizers weren't conducting evangelism crusades. They were there to convince Jesus-following gentiles to become Jewish in order to become "fully Christian." They were arguing for a blend of old and new. Included in their message was an invitation for gentile Jesus followers to come forward and be . . . not baptized . . . but circumcised!

Paul wasn't having it.

Mark my words! I, Paul, tell you that if you let yourselves be circumcised . . .[21]

Translated: If you gentiles try to sneak under the fence to participate in a covenant you weren't included in to begin with . . .

Christ will be of no value to you at all. Again I declare to every man who lets himself be circumcised that he is obligated to obey the whole law.[22]

It would be wise to pause here and allow the implications of that last statement to sink in.

Paul argues that when it comes to old and new, there can be no cherry-picking. If you pick and choose, you lose! The old covenant, like the new covenant, is an all-or-nothing proposition. As Peter learned from his encounter with Cornelius, as James affirmed at the Jerusalem Council, and as Jesus announced in his mountain message, the old and new covenants are not compatible.

They're not blendable.

They're sequential.

The old became old because it was fulfilled in Christ and replaced by something brand-spanking new.[23] The moment anyone attempts to smuggle anything old into the new, the new becomes old, and the smuggler is obligated to embrace all the old. The smuggler is obligated to slit animals' throats and stone adulterers along with Jewish converts to Christianity. The smuggler is obligated to marry his daughter off to the teenage idiot who stole her virginity.

Paul's not finished. He tosses out another analogy:

A little yeast works through the whole batch of dough.[24]

Yeast is a single-cell fungus. Add a little single-cell fungus to a dense mass of dough and, before you know it, you've got something completely different than you started with. Paul's point: a little thing can ruin the entire thing.

It only takes a small dose of the wrong thing to corrupt the whole thing. Even a pinch of old-covenant thinking or behaviors will corrupt the taste and texture of the new covenant Jesus came to establish.

He continues:

As for those agitators . . .[25]

Which agitators? The ones encouraging Jesus followers to smuggle old-covenant obligations and practices into their new-covenant Christianity.

As for those agitators, I wish they would go the whole way and emasculate themselves![26]

That's sanctified Paul talking. Imagine what he was like before Jesus recruited him!

But why the harsh language? Why get so worked up?

Paul saw what his contemporaries missed. He saw what the covenant-blending Judaizers missed. He saw what we miss. God's covenant with ancient Israel had an expiration date. It was a means to an end. The arrival of the Messiah signaled the end. This was crystal clear to Paul because, as a Pharisee, he had the courage and zeal to go where few of his contemporary, Torah-abiding, first-century Hebrews dared to go. Then he met Jesus. And he let it all go.

All of it.

We should as well.

UNHITCHED

In 2018 I preached a message from Acts 15 that created a bit of a stir. Acts 15 documents what's often referred to as the Jerusalem Council. It was there that Peter, James, and Paul finally convinced church leaders in Jerusalem that gentiles did not have to participate in God's covenant with Israel as a prerequisite to participating in God's new covenant established by Jesus. At the end of the message, I asked folks in our church if perhaps they, like Peter and Paul's adversaries, needed to *unhitch* themselves from the Old Testament as well, referring specifically to old-covenant perspectives, attitudes, and cultural values that are often smuggled into our new-covenant faith.

The statement was in part a tease for the message series to follow: The Bible for Grown-Ups, which turned out to be my favorite series. I highly recommend it, especially to those with high schoolers at home or for anyone convinced I don't preach from the Old Testament.

Folks in our churches understood and interpreted the *unhitch* comment within the context of the message. Some outside our churches did not. One way to discover what somebody means by what they say is to watch what they *do* and listen to *what else* they say. Granted, that requires time and curiosity.

Here's my point in bringing this up: I wish with all my heart that we would follow the example of the apostle Paul and *unhitch* our tone, our terminology, our approach to people, and our posture toward culture from the tone, approach, and posture toward others that permeates old-covenant narratives. I wish we, like the leaders of the Jerusalem Council, would muster the courage to distinguish our new-covenant faith from a covenant we were never included in to begin with so that we, the body of Christ, would be free to fully embrace the kingdom values, kingdom ethics, and kingdom message that Jesus "set loose in the world."[27]

King Jesus.

Lord Jesus.

Jesus who said,

"All authority in heaven and on earth has been given to me."[28]

All authority.

Moses is not our guy.

Jesus is our authority. The same Jesus who said,

"Anyone who has seen me has seen the Father."[29]

If we want to know what God is like, if we want the world to know what God is like, if we want our children and grandchildren to know what God is like, let's not introduce them to a shadow. Let's introduce them to Jesus. The reality.[30]

If you embrace the blended covenant "gospel" the apostle Paul spent his ministry arguing against, you've got some unhitching to do. I'm not referring to salvation by works.

I'm talking about a gospel draped in old-covenant values and terminology.

If you're comfortable using Old Testament warfare and conquest narratives to support your "Christian" posture toward culture and the people in it, you've got some unhitching to do. If you're more energized by the failure of your enemy than you are broken over their plight, even when it is self-inflicted, you have some unhitching to do.

If taking a political stand is causing division in your local church . . . but since you're *right*, you're convinced it's *all right* . . . you've got some unhitching to do. If making your point on social media isn't making any difference but makes it difficult for outsiders to take our faith seriously because your tone leaves readers wondering if *you* take the teaching of Jesus seriously, you've got some unhitching to do. And perhaps some apologizing.

If you think God has plans "to prosper you and not to harm you" and that he "plans to give you hope and a future," think again.[31] That's not your promise to claim. It's not your covenant. Read it in context. Do you plan to wait seventy years for God to prosper and protect you? What are you going to do in the meantime?

Your new-covenant promises are far better. Jesus promised his new-covenant disciple makers, "I am with you always . . ."[32] Beginning right now.

If you're convinced that 2 Chronicles 7:14 applies to or can be applied to the United States, you have some unhitching to do. That was a message for King Solomon after he completed the construction of the temple in Jerusalem. God was reiterating his commitment to the existing cause-and-effect covenant he'd established with the nation of Israel in the days of Moses. God doesn't have a covenant with America.

God has a covenant with you!

A better covenant.

A permanent covenant. A covenant established in his Son's blood.

When you reach back to claim what *isn't* yours to claim, you diminish the value and significance of what *is* yours to claim. Imagine the afront it is to our heavenly Father when we opt for a covenant established with the blood of goats and sheep over and against the covenant established through the blood of his Son.

Be done with the old and embrace the new. It's the covenant God created especially for you. And the *you* beside you. And the *you* that doesn't look or live like you. And the *you* that doesn't even like you. The *you* Jesus commanded you to pray for. The same *you* he died for.

STARTING OVER

As a law-abiding Pharisee, Paul was in it to win it. But on the road to Damascus, he was confronted by the King who reversed the order of things, the King who reversed Paul's way of thinking. In that moment, all Paul claimed as gain, he now saw through a different lens. Everything he had accomplished under the old covenant was nothing but dung. Stinking feces. His old-covenant currency was worthless. None of it transferred. He was bankrupt. He was starting over. He says as much in his letter to Christians in Philippi. The following passage is familiar to many of us. You may be tempted to skim it or skip it altogether. Instead, I encourage you to close your eyes for a moment and conjure up an image of young Saul of Tarsus watching in approval as Stephen is reduced to a bloody pulp outside the walls of Jerusalem.

The contrast between what Paul approved of on that day and what he aspires to in this passage is both remarkable and instructional. What follows is what new-covenant winning looks and sounds like.

Whatever were gains to me I now consider loss for the sake of Christ. What is more, I consider everything a loss because of the surpassing worth of knowing Christ Jesus my Lord, for whose sake I have lost all things. I consider them garbage, that I may gain Christ and be found in him, not having a righteousness of my own that comes from the law, but that which is through faith in Christ—the righteousness that comes from God on the basis of faith. I want to know Christ—yes, to know the power of his resurrection and participation in his sufferings, becoming like him in his death, and so, somehow, attaining to the resurrection from the dead.[33]

So what's the end game, Paul? What's the win?

> Not that I have already obtained all this, or have
> already arrived at my goal, but I press on to take
> hold of that for which Christ Jesus took hold of
> me. Brothers and sisters, I do not consider myself yet
> to have taken hold of it. But one thing I do: Forgetting
> what is behind and straining toward what is ahead,
> I press on toward the goal to *win the prize* for which
> God has called me heavenward in Christ Jesus.[34]

As you know, Paul was eventually arrested—again—
and shipped off to Rome for trial. While under house
arrest, Paul continued to correspond with church leaders
around the empire. His letters make up about half the
New Testament. The letters written by his detractors, well,
apparently nobody thought to make any copies.

According to tradition, Paul died a violent death in
Nero's Rome. As did Peter. The apostle James had been
executed sometime earlier. James the brother of Jesus, like
Stephen, was stoned outside the walls of Jerusalem.

Spineless losers.

They refused to fight back.

They went down praying.

For their enemies.

And they won!

PART THREE

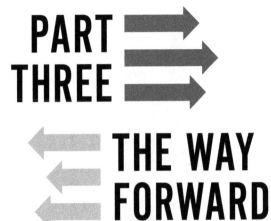

THE WAY FORWARD

CHAPTER NINE

APPLY ONLY AS DIRECTED ◀

irst-century Christians considered Jesus a living king. He was their Lord. He was not merely Lord of their prayers and worship rituals. Jesus was Lord of how they lived their lives. His authority was a living authority that held sway over every facet of life, including their posture toward imperial authority. They understood that while his kingdom was not of this world, it was *for* this world and intersected with every aspect of the physical world. Wherever his constituency found a foothold, the world became a better place.

But not because of how his followers worshiped. Not because of what they believed. The world became a better place because of how they *behaved*.

The self-serving, self-preserving, culture-warrior posture that characterizes certain streams of evangelicalism today stands in sharp and disappointing contrast with the new-covenant behavior that characterized the early church. *Believing* has become a substitute for *following*. We've been so focused on not substituting works for faith that many of us have quit working. Or in Paul's words, we quit *working out* our faith.[1]

Authentic faith does stuff.

Jesus's brother certainly thought so. According to James, faith that doesn't *accomplish* anything isn't *worth* anything. It's dead.[2] To punctuate his point, he asks his readers a rhetorical question:

> What good is it, my brothers and sisters, if someone claims to have faith but has no *deeds*?[3]

Answer?

No good.

Faith that doesn't *do* good is *no* good.

Which brings me to the point of this chapter.

COMPETING CHRISTIANS

Few Christians push back when encouraged to *walk* their *talk*, live out loud, *behave* like they *believe*. The pushback begins once we start talking specifics. Christians who stormed the Capitol on January 6 were convinced they were walking their talk. Other Christians were stunned that anyone would associate Jesus with that kind of behavior.

So who's right?

When you pass street preachers outside football stadiums, you can't help but feel a bit embarrassed by their mischaracterization of your faith. Or perhaps you're convinced I just mischaracterized our faith by suggesting they do. Many Christians are embarrassed by the "God Hates Fags" and "Hell Is for Sodomites" signs and sign holders who appear at pride rallies. But the folks holding those signs are convinced they are walking their talk and wondering why more of us don't join them.

I know why I won't. It's self-evident. To me, but not to them.

The division currently tearing churches, friends, and families apart isn't fueled by a lack of respect for our infallible text. Division begins with our less-than-infallible applications of the text.

So how do we decide how to behave?

Who gets to decide?

What does it look like and sound like to *work out* our faith? James instructs us to be *doers,* not just hearers. But *do* what?

It's an important question.

As it turns out, we don't get to choose the answer.

The answer has been prescribed and modeled for us in the New Testament. Directions are included on the label: we should take *only as directed.* We should apply *only as directed.* But something else is included on that New Testament label as well: *the outcome.* If the outcome of our application isn't as predicted, chances are we're not taking as directed.

Following Paul's instructions to Christians in Philippi

to "work out" or live out their salvation, he announces the results. When Jesus's new-covenant teaching is applied as directed, here's what can be expected:

> . . . so that you may become *blameless* and *pure*, "children of God without *fault* in a warped and crooked generation." Then you will *shine* among them like stars in the sky.[4]

Being right, even believing right, doesn't make us shine. Applying right is what makes us shine.

I'm afraid we've lost our shine.

We aren't shining because we aren't applying our faith *as directed*.[5] Consequently, while we believe differently than outsiders, we don't behave much different. Most notable and noticeable is we don't *react* much differently when things don't go our way.

Our actions and reactions undermine the credibility of our faith claims. Outsiders aren't about to take our faith seriously as long as they wonder if we do. If Paul is correct, if we aren't shining, we aren't *doing* it right. We aren't applying our faith right. We aren't applying it *as directed*. Instead, we've painted crosses on the means and methods employed by the kingdoms of this world, and the contrast isn't apparent.

For the most part.

But every once in a while, a little light shines through. Occasionally, somebody's unusual reaction slices through the darkness in such a way that everybody stops to take notice. In those moments, we're reminded that the light of Christ cannot be overcome by darkness. In those moments, the light of Christ has its intended effect. If what has become the exception rather than the rule ever became the rule, our nation would change.

For the better.

ON DISPLAY

In November 2021, the Justice Department announced a settlement with families of those fatally shot in 2015 at the Emanuel African Methodist Episcopal Church in Charleston, South Carolina.[6] No doubt you remember that horrific racially motivated mass shooting. Nine African American parishioners were gunned down by an avowed white supremacist during a Bible study, including a state senator and the church's senior pastor.

Mass shootings don't garner the attention or outrage they once did. We've become somewhat desensitized by the sheer volume. But not this one. As horrific as the murders were, what transpired in a Charleston County courtroom two years later was what took our national breath away.

During sentencing, survivors and relatives of the victims could speak directly to Dylann Roof, the man who murdered family members and friends, then laughed and bragged about it later. One by one, they forgave the man who gunned down loved ones because of the color of their skin. Anthony Thompson, whose wife, Myra, was shot and killed at point-blank range, looked his wife's murderer in the eyes and said, "I forgive you and my family forgives you. But we would like to take this opportunity to ask you to repent. To repent. To confess and give your life to the One who matters most—Christ."[7]

Pause.

Mr. Thompson invited Dylann Roof to make a decision that according to Thompson's way of thinking would enable Roof to share heaven with the folks he murdered.

Including his wife.

Are you kidding?

Wouldn't "I hope you rot in hell" be more appropriate?

Perhaps.

No doubt that would have reflected Roof's sentiment two years earlier as he calmly pulled out his weapon, stared into the eyes of his victims, and pulled the trigger. Over and over and over. But Mr. Thompson and the other folks who addressed Roof were nothing like Dylann Roof. They weren't in it to win it. They had already lost so much. But they weren't there for payback. Justice was being served. But that didn't bring their loved ones back.

The posture Anthony Thompson embraced went far beyond what was expected. He reached beyond what the law required. He wasn't being a good citizen. He wasn't even being a good Christian. He was following Jesus.

But he wasn't finished.

"We would like to take this opportunity to ask you to . . . confess and give your life to the One who matters most—Christ, so he can change you. He can change your ways no matter what happens to you."[8]

Empathy? For his wife's murderer? His final statement:

"And you, you will be okay."[9]

Breathtaking. At multiple levels.

A Black man, with his own personal history of navigating growing up Black in the South, forgives and promises to pray for a white nationalist Nazi who gunned down his wife and friends because of the color of their skin.

What a loser.

(That was hard to type.)

You know better.

We all know better. Why can't we be *that* better?

WHAT ARE LITTLE GIRLS WORTH?

American gymnast Rachael Denhollander was the first woman to publicly accuse USA Gymnastics team doctor Larry Nassar of sexual assault.[10] In 2016 she alleged that he repeatedly engaged in horrific and humiliating behavior when she was his patient. Her actions paved the way for over 265 women to come forward with their own accounts of abuse.[11] These included Olympic gold medalists McKayla

Maroney, Aly Raisman, and Simone Biles.[12] Their courage and tenacity brought long overdue attention to a pattern of sexual abuse associated with USA Gymnastics. The organization's self-protecting culture had allowed an evil man to harm hundreds of young women and girls over the course of many years. But no more.

In 2018 a Michigan court found Nassar guilty on charges of child pornography and sexual assault. While Denhollander was the first to accuse Nassar, she was the last of over 150 victims to confront Nassar in the courtroom during the sentencing phase of his trial. When her turn finally came, she addressed her initial remarks to the men and women in the courtroom.

"How much is a little girl worth?" she asked.[13]

Denhollander's question hung in the air. Referring to the other women who came forward with their own horrific stories, she continued:

"I submit to you that these children are worth everything."

Then Denhollander addressed Nassar directly:

"In our early hearings, you brought your Bible into the courtroom and you have spoken of praying for forgiveness. And so it is on that basis that I appeal to you. If you have read the Bible you carry, you know the definition of sacrificial love portrayed is of God himself loving so sacrificially that he gave up everything to pay a penalty for the sin he did not commit.

By his grace, I, too, choose to love this way."

She continued:

"Should you ever reach the point of truly facing what you have done, the guilt will be crushing. And that is what makes the gospel of Christ so sweet. Because it extends grace and hope and mercy where none should be found. And it will be there for you. I pray you experience the soul-crushing weight of guilt so you may someday experience true repentance and true forgiveness from God, which you need far more than forgiveness from me—though I extend that to you as well."

Silence.

Everyone in the courtroom was stunned. If that's the first you knew of this exchange, it's okay to use your shirt sleeve.

If Rachael Denhollander had stood up in that Michigan courtroom and spewed years of pent-up venom reserved for a day like that one, should it ever arrive, no one would have blamed her. I imagine there were days she would have done exactly that had the opportunity presented itself. But on that day, Jesus, not anger, was her Lord. Jesus, rather than vindication, compelled her. On that day, her past did not define her. She didn't come to win.

She came to forgive.

She brought the kingdom of God to a courtroom, and there wasn't anything anybody could do about it. She showed up with the sword of the Spirit, the shield of faith, and the wrecking ball of forgiveness. She was one of those blameless and pure "children of God without fault in a warped and crooked generation."[14] Rachael Denhollander shone like a star in the sky.

"By his grace, I, too, choose to love this way."

Love? Really? That's all you got, Rachael? We thought you were a competitor.

How weak.

How strong.

Wanna know why you teared up reading Rachael's account? You were blinded by the shine.

Let's shine.

PARALLEL WORLDS

The events involving Dylann Roof and Larry Nassar share several things in common. One is of particular importance for our discussion. Both incidents involve intervention by government agencies. And rightly so. Laws were broken. The defendants would go to prison regardless of what Rachael

Denhollander or Anthony Thompson said or didn't say. Also relevant, Rachael Denhollander was the first woman to publicly accuse Nassar of sexual assault. As a Christian, Denhollander appealed to the government for protection from an adversary. The apostle Paul did the same thing.[15] But both Denhollander and Paul maintained a Christlike posture throughout their appeals. This is the new-covenant pattern for Jesus followers. New Testament authors are in agreement that government was established by God for the purpose of administering judgment.[16] Referring to government officials, Paul wrote,

> They are God's servants, agents of wrath to bring punishment on the wrongdoer.[17]

Or as Jonathan Leeman says,

> We acknowledge that God gave government to humanity for the purposes of peace and flourishing.[18]

> God gave the sword of government to all creation because of the fall.[19]

Our current justice system may be the best possible *system* given the limitations of time and space. But no system is better than the people involved. Mistakes will be made. Justice will be delayed. Power, reputation, and connections will always threaten the integrity of due process. But the

New Testament is clear. A corrupt or inept criminal justice system does not represent an off-ramp for followers of Jesus. Injustice is not an excuse to abandon our new-covenant mandate. Delayed justice—and even injustice at times—can be the backdrop against which the light of Christ and the light of his followers shines brightest.

Don't forget.

Our faith is anchored to a miscarriage of justice. The worst possible thing happened to the best possible person.

THE QUESTION

Back to where this chapter began.

What did Paul mean by *working out* our faith? What was James referring to when he instructed first-century followers *to do* and not just *listen?* Do what? What were the *good deeds* Jesus was referring to when he said,

Let your light shine before others, that they may see your *good deeds* and glorify your Father in heaven.[20]

What was Peter referring to when he instructed Jesus followers to live *good lives* among their pagan neighbors?[21] What does a *good life* look and sound like? According to Peter, a *good life*, whatever that is, has the power to "silence the ignorant talk of foolish people."[22]

What does it look and sound like to *apply* our faith as *directed* by our *Savior?*

The short answer: It looks and sounds a lot like losing.

Jesus's disciples certainly thought so. While on their way to Jerusalem, where Jesus would become the biggest loser, the disciples were arguing about which of them would hold the second and third spots in his soon-to-be established kingdom.

Remember what Jesus said in response?

Most Christians don't.

It's epic.

"You know that those who are regarded as rulers of the Gentiles lord it over them, and their high officials exercise authority over them."[23]

Of course they knew that. Everybody knew that. It's why they were jockeying for position. When Jesus won, they wanted to be close to the winner!

The next four words out of Jesus's mouth are . . . startling.[24] Disarming. Unsettling. His next four words flip the power script. Jesus redefines winning. And losing. His next four words are directed at me and folks like me. At you and folks like you. We know how the power game is played. We're aware of the benefits and perks that come with position and title. Our assumption is, if it comes *to* us, it must be *for* us. But not in the upside-down kingdom of King Jesus. So Jesus stared 'em all down and declared,

"Not so with you."[25]

Implication: When it comes to opportunity, privilege, title, and position, forget everything you've learned and ignore what you've seen modeled. I'm introducing a new model.

"Instead . . ."[26]

Read: In stark contrast to how you've seen it done.

> "Instead, whoever wants to become great among you must be your servant, and whoever wants to be first must be slave of all."[27]

Servant? Slave? Of all? That's moving in the wrong direction. That's going down, not up. That's more lose than win.

That's not *great*.

That's . . . humiliating.

That's why we resist.

We want to be prophets calling out evil and calling down curses. We want to be warriors of Christ, bathed in the blood of our enemies (figuratively speaking). We want the nations to tremble. We want to be ancient Israel (minus the inconvenient dietary restrictions) retaking the promised land!

What we don't want to be is followers of Jesus. That requires going to the back of the line. Here's how he closed out his roadside chat:

"For even the Son of Man did not come to be served, but to serve, and to give his life as a ransom for many."[28]

When Jesus finished, they continued on their way to Jerusalem, where the apostles realized he was not kidding. He was planning to lose. When that became inconveniently and threateningly evident, they all unfollowed him. Mark, who preserved Peter's account of what happened in the garden of Gethsemane, didn't hold back. With Peter's permission, he exposed Jesus's closest friends as users and cowards.

Then everyone deserted him and fled.[29]

Why?

Because they witnessed firsthand what our *Made in America* faith makes it difficult for us to see. Jesus did not come to be served but to serve and to literally, painfully, selflessly give his life away. He worked his way to the back of the line. He was crucified by the winners between two other losers.

No wonder we're content to believe rather than follow.

"Believers" can have it both ways.

"Believers" get to go to new-covenant heaven when they die while determining for themselves what the Christian faith looks, acts, and sounds like in the meantime. And what does *Made in America* Christianity look, act, and sound like?

Winning.

But Jesus had something to say about that as well:

"For whoever wants to save their life . . ."[30]

Wait for it.

. . . will lose it . . .

In the end, winners lose.

. . . but whoever loses their life for me and for the gospel will save it.

In the end, the savers are the losers. And the losers are the savers.

"What good is it for someone to gain the whole world, yet forfeit their soul?"[31]

Answer: No good.

"Whoever wants to be my disciple must *deny* themselves and take up their cross and *believe in* me."

Nope.

"Whoever wants to be my disciple must *deny* themselves and take up their cross and *follow* me.[32]

Follow him where?

To the back of the line.

With all the other losers. Folks like Rachael Denhollander and Anthony Thompson.

So what exactly do *doers* do? What are the *good works* Jesus referred to? What are the good works that cause people to stop, stare, and make the connection between us and our Father in heaven? Or, to put it simply, what does following Jesus look, act, and sound like?

Paul provides us with the clearest answer.

Maybe too clear.

THE LAW OF CHRIST

As we discussed in chapter 7, just before his arrest, Jesus gave his disciples a new command.

"My command is this: Love each other as I have loved you."[33]

Much of Jesus's teaching was actionable. But his action items were simply applications of his new-covenant command.

For example, removing the log out of your eye before pointing out the speck in your brother's eye is how you love your brother. Leaving your pigeon at the altar while you return home to make things right with your sister is how you love your sister. Loving your enemy is, well, loving your enemy.

You get the point.

Everything Jesus instructed his first-century followers to do was simply first-century application of his single new command. If the church ever chooses to reestablish that single command as the standard against which all our behavior is evaluated, we may regain our shine.

And that brings us to the apostle Paul.

Paul did for first-century gentile Jesus followers what Jesus did for his Galilean and Judean followers. Paul applied Jesus's *new command* to his predominantly postpagan audiences. But Paul didn't refer to Jesus's new command as *Jesus's new command*. He gave it a title that made more sense to and carried more weight with gentiles. He referred to Jesus's new command as

The law of Christ.[34]

Did you know Christ had his own law?
He did. Still does.

APPLICATION LIST

Like Jesus, Paul provided his gentile audiences with dozens of applications of the law of Christ. They're scattered throughout his letters. If you want to know what *doers do* and how *followers follow*, Paul gives us plenty to work with. But all his instructions and imperatives fit neatly under, and flow directly from, Jesus's command to love as he loved. Read Paul's letters with that in mind and the connection will jump off the page.

To Christians in the province of Galatia, Paul wrote,

Carry each other's burdens . . .

Why?

. . . and in this way you will fulfill the *law of Christ*.[35]

Carrying someone's burdens is how you love someone with a burden. Why should we care? Why should we carry? Because Christ carried our burden. This is what doers do and how followers follow.

To gentile Christians living in the port city of Ephesus, Paul wrote,

Get rid of all bitterness, rage and anger, brawling and slander, along with every form of malice. Be kind and compassionate to one another, forgiving each other . . .[36]

Good advice.
But *why*?

Why should we be kind to the unkind and compassionate to the uncompassionate? Why forgive? Forgiveness is a gift to the guilty. Anticipating our question, Paul cites his source:

... just as in Christ God forgave you.[37]

We are to do for others what Christ did for us. Refusing to respond with rage, anger, and slander when someone has earned a dose of rage, anger, and slander is what doers do.

It's how followers follow.

To the point of this book, for Jesus followers, there is no place for rage, brawling, slander, or any form of malice at any time, for any reason. There's no such thing as righteous slander. Or holy brawling. Those are the means and methods of the kingdoms of this world. Jesus didn't use 'em. Paul abandoned them. We should follow their example. As Russell Moore points out,

> Someone with an unhealthy craving for controversy can always convince himself that he's a warrior for Christ—instead of a captive to his passions.[38]

As Jesus followers, we are instructed not to be captive to *our* passions. Our lives should reflect the passions of our Savior. He was indeed passionate. But he was not fearful.

Admittedly, it's difficult not to be captive to our passions when it appears everything we value is under assault and that if we don't fight to protect it, we'll lose it. The good news is—and the advantage we have over our first-century brothers and sisters is—we can express our political, civil, and in some instances religious and moral passions legally and privately. We choose our own local, state, and national representatives. We aren't subject to *they the empire*. We have an opportunity and obligation to participate in *we the people*.

If we truly care about America and our fellow Americans, we should consistently do two things. We should apply our faith as directed by our Savior, and we should vote our law-of-Christ-informed conscience every chance we get. Regarding how we apply our faith, Paul wrote,

Follow God's example, therefore, as dearly loved children and walk in *the way of love* . . .[39]

"The way of love." Sounds romantic. But there's another "just as" around the bend.

. . . *just as* Christ loved us and gave himself up for us as a fragrant offering and sacrifice to God.[40]

The way of love sounds soft until we consider that it culminated in a man hanging from a cross drenched in his own body fluids. Embracing the full scope of crucifixion removes any modern misconceptions regarding the way of love. Christian behavior—all Christian behavior—should be informed by the sacrificial love of Jesus.

APPLICATION GUIDE

Jesus's new-covenant command—or as Paul refers to it, the law of Christ—serves as a north star for Christian behavior. Both Jesus's and Paul's instructions and imperatives are simply applications of that single, overarching command. We can debate *what it looks like* to love other people the way Christ loves us. But we don't get to decide *whether* to love others the way God through Christ loved us. That's decided for us. It's been modeled for us. It's been prescribed to us.

The law of Christ should inform our consciences and stand guard over our hearts and mouths. The law of Christ should govern our responses, actions, reactions, and priorities. The law of Christ is how followers from every nation and in every generation discover what following looks and sounds like in their cultural context. The law of Christ should compel us to pause and ask questions like:

What would it look like to love this person . . . these people . . . the way Christ loved me?

What would a Christlike response look like? Sound like?

How could I put this person first?

What would it look like in this situation to go to the back of the line?

When I teach this material, I often end with this:

When you're not sure what to say or do,
ask what loves requires of you.

That's what *faith expressing itself through love* looks and sounds like. That's how followers follow. That's what doers do. That's how the love of God behaves.

THE GREAT EXPECTATION

So now you know.

Maybe you already knew.

Turns out, we aren't the only ones who know. Do you know how people who don't subscribe to our faith expect us to behave?

Like Jesus.

The nerve! Right?

Actually, don't they have every right?

Don't they have every right to expect those of us who claim to be Jesus followers to actually follow his example? To act and, perhaps most importantly, to react as Jesus did? Our responses and reactions say more about the sincerity and authenticity of our faith than anything else, certainly more than our sermons, songs, and creeds. Or as Russell Moore says,

> If people reject the church because they reject Jesus and the gospel, we should be saddened but not surprised.
>
> But what happens when people reject the church because they think *we* reject Jesus and the gospel? . . . And what if people don't leave the church because

they disapprove of Jesus, but because they've read the Bible and have come to the conclusion that the church itself would disapprove of Jesus? That's a crisis.[41]

It is indeed.

I'm convinced a significant percentage of evangelicals would, in fact, disapprove of Jesus. He was too passive. He refused to fight back. He wasn't in it to win it.

Pilate certainly assumed that to be the case. You remember Pilate?

The gospel writer John, who took copious notes and had unnamed sources in unusual places, described a short conversation between Jesus and Governor Pilate. By the time this conversation took place, Jesus had been beaten, crowned with thorns, and flogged.

Picture it.

Governor Pilate had the power. He was holding all the cards. Passive, turn-the-other-cheek Jesus was at his mercy. Or so Pilate thought. But something was wrong. Jesus should have been on his knees begging for mercy, promising anything . . . anything to avoid the horror of crucifixion. But Jesus wouldn't even answer Pilate's questions. Exasperated, Pilate said,

"You refuse to speak to me! Don't you realize I have the *authority* to release you and the *authority* to crucify you?"[42]

To which Jesus (essentially) replied,

> "No, you don't. Somebody does. But it's not you."[43]

He could have gone on to say,

> But I do have some good news for you, Governor. History will not forget you. Your name will be spoken in places the hobnail boots of your legions have yet to leave their imprint. Your name will be documented in the most widely read literature of all time, but not for your military prowess or your accomplishments as governor of Judea.
>
> Governor Pilate, you will be a footnote in *my* story. For all of time you will be the Roman governor who sanctioned the execution of a king. The King to whom future Roman kings will bow.

I'm convinced many evangelicals would choose someone like Pilate over Jesus. Large and in charge. With armed guards standing at the ready. In it to win it. But in the end, Pilate is reduced to a footnote in the story of the passive day laborer from Galilee who changed the world.

IMAGINE

Once upon a time, the "love one another" behavior of the church stood in sharp contrast to the "bite and devour" one another behavior of the pagan world. What was true then should be true today. The "others first" way of Jesus appeals to something deep in the soul of every man, woman, and child. We all want to be included, honored, valued, recognized, and loved.

Imagine a world where people were skeptical of what we believed but envious of how well we treated one another. Imagine a world where unbelievers were anxious to hire, vote for, work for, work with, and live next door to Christians because of how well we treated one another and how well we treated them.

We can choose to follow Jesus.

We do not get to choose what following Jesus looks and sounds like.

It's been prescribed. It's on the label.

It looks and sounds like Jesus.

CHAPTER TEN

MOST IMPORTANT NOW

When Garrett, our second-born, came along, baby monitors were still a relatively new addition to the vast array of parenting paraphernalia. The technology was limited to audio. But it was a big improvement on running upstairs every few hours to check on the baby.

Late one evening as Sandra and I were cleaning up after dinner with friends, our conversation was interrupted by a hacking cough blaring through the plastic speaker on the kitchen counter. We rushed upstairs to find Garrett, who was about eighteen months old at the time, in the throes of a coughing fit unlike anything we had seen or heard before. We did what we knew, which wasn't much, but his cough worsened, and we could see he was having a difficult time catching his breath.

We were terrified.

I called 9-1-1 while Sandra held Garrett and prayed.

In minutes, a fire truck pulled up outside our house. My first thought was, *Oh no, they think our house is on fire!* Turns out, a fire truck is protocol.

The EMTs weren't far behind. When they reached the

front door, Sandra herded them toward the kitchen, where I was holding Garrett. They set down their equipment and the older of the two reached out to take him, at which point I stepped back and asked the question any responsible parent would ask before handing their child to a skilled emergency medical technician:

"Republican or Democrat?"

If you're a parent, you get it. You would never trust the health of your child to someone without first discovering which way they leaned politically.

Right?

Of course not.

I didn't care about their politics. I cared about their *competency*.

Why?

This was an *emergency*.

Do you know what happens during an emergency? I'm sure you do. But you haven't given it much thought, which is understandable because during an emergency, we don't give anything much thought other than the emergency. During an emergency, we don't process information the way we do in nonemergency situations. During an emergency, what's *actually* most important *becomes* most important.

During an emergency, priorities get reshuffled. What's most important makes its way to the top of the list without any conscious effort on our part.

But . . .

Apart from an emergency, what's most important is rarely a priority.

Apart from an emergency, our pursuit of happiness takes priority. In the church, our theological, ecumenical distinctives—along with a variety of cultural and political soapbox issues—become the priority. None of which are *most* important and many of which we've allowed to divide us. All of which sets us up to be divvied up into opposing political and cultural corners.

The American church is in a state of emergency.

But currently, we are too distracted to notice. We have continued to allow ourselves to be divided by secondary concerns while what should be our biggest concern continues to go unaddressed—namely, division. Division is the threat. Division is the enemy. Because of its size, a united church in the United States with all its beautiful cultural diversity would have the influence necessary to move the nation back toward the middle, the place where problems are actually solved. The middle, where defenses come down, experiences are shared, and people are inclined to listen.

To one another.

Pause to consider the non-Great-Commission-critical issues we've allowed to divide us—everything from climate change to critical race theory to COVID, masks, and vaccines. Two doses, three doses, no doses, who knowses? Why . . . why . . . why would we, the light of the world, the salt of the earth, the hands and feet of Jesus, allow ourselves to be baited into debates and divided over questions about which we all have opinions informed by partial and skewed information.

I know . . .

You're the exception. You have the facts.

Perhaps you do.

Share 'em.

But don't share 'em in a way that undermines the *unity* of the body of Christ. If you do, even if you're right, you're part of the problem. You are ignoring the *real* emergency. Five years from now, our "everybody needs to know" opinions will be all but irrelevant and forgotten. But the damage to the body will be done.

And you will have contributed.

I know that's not your intention. But direction, not intention, determines destination. The nation is moving in a dangerous direction. But instead of leading, the church is following. We're following because we're divided. We're divided because we've allowed ourselves to be divided.

Unity will become the priority only if we are willing to acknowledge that a *lack of unity* signals *an emergency.* When that happens, the church in the United States will set aside our partisan differences along with a host of other mostly irrelevant points of disagreement and serve as the conscience of our nation. Or as my friend Dr. Crawford Loritts said over dinner not long ago,

> "The church will serve as the visible destination to which the culture should eventually arrive."[1]

Or as Dr. Tony Evans put it almost forty years ago during my graduate school days,

> "The church will serve as a commercial for a coming attraction."

Commercials make you lean in. Look forward to. Plan to be a part of. I'm not sure what we're currently advertising. But if church attendance is any indication, apparently it's not all that attractive.

So what should we do?

To contextualize words penned in the first century by the author of Hebrews:

> Since we are surrounded by such a great cloud of witnesses . . .

Perhaps the apostle Paul is watching? Stephen? Peter? James?

> . . . let us throw off *everything* that *hinders* and the sin that so easily entangles.[2]

For such a time as this, could we not throw off anything and everything that entangles and divides us? Could we not rid ourselves of everything that trips us up?

> And let us run with perseverance the race marked out for us.[3]

The race marked out for us two-thousand-plus years before a handful of brave patriots decided that life, liberty, and the pursuit of happiness marked out our race.

Fixing our eyes on . . .

What you stare at determines what you gravitate toward.

Our division is proof that we're not all staring—and thus not moving—in the same direction. Our eyes are *fixed* on something. But it ain't what the author of Hebrews suggests. Our eyes have been fixed on *winning*. Winning fueled by fear of *losing* our freedom. Losing our rights. Losing our country. And if we continue moving in our current divided direction, our misplaced fear will fuel what we fear most. We could lose all the aforementioned.

We have lost our fear of division, and consequently, we have lost our voice and our influence. Thus, we've lost our best opportunity to preserve and protect the liberty many are so afraid of losing. Our division fuels the thing we fear most. So, in the words of the author of Hebrews, let's fix our eyes on and orient our lives around

Jesus, the pioneer and perfecter of faith.[4]

When our eyes are fixed on Jesus as portrayed in the Gospels, his life, his posture, his responses and reactions will inform and conform us. If we collectively turn our eyes upon Jesus and "look full in his wonderful face," perhaps then the "things of this earth" will at last "grow strangely dim in the light of his glory and grace." Then, to paraphrase Crawford again:

> Our faith will no longer be reduced to a point of reference. It will become the context for our entire lives.[5]

Unity of *purpose* is essential to the body of Christ. If you are a member, unity must become important to you as well, or you will contribute to rather than respond to the current emergency.

OUR RESPONSIBILITY

The path of least resistance is always to complain about everything and do nothing about anything. In this season of my life, it's tempting. I can complain with the best of 'em, and perhaps like you, I have an opinion about everything. And everybody. So yeah, it would be easy to sit back and talk back to the television. It would be easy to surround myself with people who are like me, who like me, and who experience the world like me.

Unlike me, you may have opted to shut it all out. No more cable news for you. No more Facebook, Instagram, or Twitter. You're out! And you don't miss it. You don't want to hear about it. You didn't even want to read this book. I get it. Once upon a time people were only aware of what was happening in their communities. Now we're aware of everything, everywhere, all the time, and it's too much. It's overwhelming. Since you can't take it all on, it's easier just to shut it all out.

But . . .

While complaining about everything but doing nothing may pass as a suitable option for twenty-first-century "Christians," it is not an option for those of us who wake up every day committed to following Jesus. He did not leave that option open to us. If you've opted to tune it all out, I get it. But while unawareness is bliss, for Jesus followers, unawareness is a swing and a miss because you've never been bothered by or inspired to respond to human suffering you're unaware of. You've never engaged with a problem you didn't know about. Neither option is open to us. We can't shut it all out, nor can we take it all on. We can't do nothing and complain about everything.

Our responses to the world around us have been prescribed to us and modeled for us by our Savior. As followers, we have a responsibility. Left and Right. Black, Brown, and White. We, collectively, have a responsibility. The good news is, it's not our responsibility to solve the world's problems. We will never agree on how to solve the world's problems. Or our nation's problems. Let's be honest.

Some of us can't solve our own problems.

You're confident you would know what to do if you were president. But you're not sure what to do with your eight-year-old. Or your eighteen-year-old. Fortunately, Jesus has not commissioned us to solve the world's problems. Turns out, he didn't attempt to solve them all either.

DISTURBING

Follow Jesus through the Gospels and you bump into something surprising and disturbing. While Jesus often stopped to meet the immediate needs of individuals, he posited no permanent solutions for any of society's big problems.

Not one.

On purpose.

Because he came for a different purpose.

Jesus refused to be dragged into or tricked into taking sides on civic, social, and what we would consider political matters. He made no effort to fix *the system*. And there was so much that needed to be fixed. It was a broken justice system unduly influenced by lobbyists representing the interests of the temple that led to his execution. Yet even as a victim of a broken justice system, Jesus refused to comment on the injustice of the system. Instead, he looked Governor Pilate in the eye and assured him that *he* wasn't the one running this show. Stranger still, from a cross he did not deserve to be nailed to, Jesus forgave the folks who nailed him there. Jesus refused to address the system because he came to address something else—the hearts behind the systems. The hearts that created, defended, and profited off the system.

206 ⇒ The Way Forward

The Gospels document interactions between Jesus and two tax collectors: Matthew and Zacchaeus. The system used to determine what taxes were owed, when they were owed, and how they were paid was extraordinarily corrupt. This was due in part to the fact that the system, like most ancient systems, was virtually impossible to monitor. But Jesus neither condemned the system, nor did he offer suggestions on how to improve it. Instead, he addressed two participants. He invited Matthew to follow him and invited himself to Zacchaeus's house for lunch. While Jesus made no effort to change how taxes were collected, these two encounters changed two tax collectors.

And *that* was his purpose.

As far as we know, neither Matthew nor Zacchaeus attempted to change the system. Zacchaeus changed his approach. Matthew changed careers.

In another missed opportunity, Jesus was asked to heal a Roman centurion's slave. He accepted the invitation but failed to condemn or even comment on slavery. During his final visit to Jerusalem, the Pharisees provided Jesus with the perfect opportunity to call out both the injustice of the imperial tax code as well as the horror inflicted on Judeans by their Roman occupiers.[6] Again, he refused to take the bait. He refused to choose sides.

Why?

Obviously, he was a coward. He was afraid of losing followers. He didn't want to offend anybody. So he refused to take a stand.

Sheesh.

When a woman caught in adultery is taken against her will to the temple and placed at Jesus's feet for judgment, how does he respond? Instead of addressing the system that justified this miscarriage of justice, Jesus addressed the hypocrisy festering in the hearts of the woman's accusers. He addressed the source of the problem.

When the woman's accusers eventually left, Jesus addressed her heart issue as well. He doesn't excuse her behavior. He doesn't attempt to assuage her guilt. He doesn't take sides. He is as direct with her as he was with her accusers: "Leave your life of sin."[7]

Everything that disturbs you about America originated in the hearts of Americans.

Everything.

I say that with certainty because Jesus said it with such clarity:

"The things that come out of a person's mouth *come from the heart*."[8]

Are you disturbed by people talking *at* rather than *to* one another? Are you bothered by the condescending tone and dehumanizing terminology that characterizes so much of our national conversation? That's not a political problem. That doesn't change or improve if your candidate wins. If your candidate wins, it might get worse. Jesus labeled this behavior a heart problem.

"For out of the heart come evil thoughts—murder, adultery, sexual immorality, theft, false testimony, slander."[9]

Everything that disturbs you about our nation, along with everything that disturbs you about *you,* can be directly or indirectly linked to that short list. Jesus caps it off with this:

"These are what defile a person."[10]

These are what defile a nation.

Everything that disturbs you about the United States emanates from the sinful, selfish, self-centered, appetite-fueled, fear-driven condition of the human heart. Our government can *protect* us from it. But our government is powerless to do anything about it. No system of government, no political platform, no bill, law, or mandate can change a human heart. Aleksandr Solzhenitsyn said it well,

"The line dividing good and evil cuts through the heart of every human being."[11]

So why allow ourselves to be entangled by and divided by secondary concerns when we are stewards of *the message* that has the potential to make the most difference?

Jesus knew better. We can do better. We must do better.

Imagine what would happen if the church refused to

take sides politically, abandoned our culture war mentality, and fearlessly, directly, and politically incorrectly addressed matters of the heart. What if we realigned our teaching, preaching, and discipleship around Jesus and his new-covenant command? Nothing highlights the garbage collecting in the recesses of our hearts faster than holding our actions and reactions up against Jesus's command to love as he loved. Nothing clarifies where we are, where we aren't, and where we should be with more precision than asking, *What does Jesus's love for me require of me?*

BUT THERE'S MORE

While Jesus refused to fix or even address the systemic inequalities rampant in first-century Judea, Samaria, and Galilee, he never missed an opportunity to address an immediate need—regardless of whose it was or what created the need to begin with. As John observed, Jesus was the personification of grace and truth. He did not attempt to balance grace and truth. That's what we do. Jesus was *all* grace and *all* truth *all* the time.

He never dumbed down the truth. He never turned down the grace. It was confusing at times. It caused him to look inconsistent at times. But he knew what we must rediscover: that grace and truth is the way forward. John, who grew up on the teaching of Moses, underscored the unique approach introduced by his resurrected rabbi:

For the law was given through Moses; grace and truth came through Jesus Christ.[12]

Jesus didn't directly address the system, but he never missed an opportunity to address the physical and emotional needs of those hurt by the system and left floundering in its wake. Over and over, Jesus stopped what he was doing and came to the aid of the suffering, whether Judean, Galilean, Samaritan, or Roman. Slaves and slave owners. The righteous and the unrighteous.

As grace and truth, Jesus addressed matters of the heart while addressing the needs of those whose lives had been shattered by their own corrupted hearts as well as the heartlessness of others. In doing so, he revealed what God is like.

"Anyone who has seen me has seen the Father."[13]

Implication: "Anyone who has seen me work has seen the Father at work. Want to know what is most important to your heavenly Father? Watch me. Listen to me. Then follow me."

Want to see systemic change? Want to see America become great as Jesus defined great? Then somebody must stand apart from the legislative, executive, judicial, and political to address the hearts of those elected and selected to fill these essential and critical roles.

We are that somebody.

Somebody must model compassion, generosity, and empathy for those negatively impacted by the consequences of their own decisions as well as those suffering from the unintended consequences of imperfect systems.

We are that somebody as well.

HANDS ON

It should not be lost on us that Jesus's last act of service before his arrest and execution was washing his disciples' feet. Jesus washed their feet even though they were about to get dirty again.

In ancient times, foot care was the most subservient task performed by a household servant or slave. While ancient teachers and rabbis often expected their disciples to function as servants, foot washing was considered too demeaning for a disciple. So when Jesus stood up during the Passover meal, removed his rabbinic robe, and wrapped a towel around his waist . . . we can only imagine the emotion in the room.

This could not happen. They knew what those hands were capable of. They had witnessed the power of his touch. Lord or no Lord, he would not touch—much less wash—their dirty feet.

But he did.

It takes a long time to wash twelve pairs of feet. Most of that time was spent watching him wash the other eleven pairs of feet.

Fishermen's feet.

A former tax collector's feet.

A traitor's feet.

Perhaps we should pause for a moment and let that sink in. Jesus got down on his knees in front of Judas and washed his feet.

A thread of unhealthy competition divided some men from the others in that room. Perhaps Peter objected to Jesus's washing his feet because he would never consider washing the feet of others gathered around that table.

When their baptism of humiliation came to an end, Jesus stood, put his rabbinical robe back on, and returned to his reserved seat of honor. And nobody said a word.

> "Do you understand what I have done *for you*?" he asked them.[14]

"For us? No."
"To us, yes."

> "You call me 'Teacher' and 'Lord,' and rightly so, for that is what I am. Now that I, your Lord and Teacher, have washed your feet, you also should wash one another's feet."

Even though they will get dirty again.

> "I have set you an example that you should do as I have done for you."

This was Jesus's way of punctuating and illustrating the degree to which he expected them—and us—to embrace and live out his new-covenant command. To love others the way Jesus loved them would require them to get their hands dirty. With other people's dirt. They knew from experience what we miss in this emotional encounter with their Lord. Washing one another's feet ensured that their differences would not *divide* them.

Because . . .

> You can't wash feet from a distance.
> You can't wash feet from an elevated position.
> You can't even wash feet eye to eye.

"Very truly I tell you, no servant is greater than his master, nor is a messenger greater than the one who sent him. Now that you know these things, you will be blessed if you do them."

DISTANCE DIVIDES

The further we are from a problem, the simpler the solution appears to be. But when we get close, when we are confronted with the complexity disguised by the distance, when we are forced to consider someone's current reality and context—in those moments our well-rehearsed, simplistic, politically-informed solutions become mostly irrelevant.

Sometimes embarrassing. When we get close enough and stoop down low enough to wash feet, we usually have an "Oh!" moment.

Oh! I've always assumed . . .

Oh! I thought people like that were . . .

Oh! I never took into account . . .

Oh! I didn't know . . .

"Oh!" moments don't resolve disagreements. They resolve division and provide us with vision. "Oh!" moments lead us to *the question* that bridges the divide better than any other:

What can I do to help?

Or to leverage the apostle Paul's words:

How can I carry your burden?

Remember, carrying someone's burden is not merely a random *act of kindness*.

Carrying another's burden is how we fulfill the *law of Christ*.[15]

It's not an add-on. It's essential. It's what should characterize us. When we shoulder the burden of those unlike us, we always discover there's less not to like. We are less critical. Less judgmental. Less sure of our solutions. We're reminded of the common ground, the common struggle, the common hopes and fears shared by every image bearer.

THE BRIDGE

In an emergency, what's most important becomes most important. Jesus told us what's most important for his body: unity. He left us a single command to ensure that we moved and worked together despite our differences. "By *this* everyone will know . . ."[16]

If we are willing to orient our lives around Jesus's new-covenant command, it will serve as the bridge between our differences. It will bridge our political differences as well as our dissimilar life experiences. It will serve as a bridge between our disagreements regarding how problems should be solved and how issues should be addressed. Political and ideological alignment is not a prerequisite for carrying one another's burdens. I can love you the way Jesus loved me regardless of who you voted for. We can wash one another's feet without knowing where those feet have been or where they are headed next. We can—we must—wash one another's feet knowing that they will, in fact, get dirty again.

Washing feet doesn't solve problems. But it keeps us close.

If we choose to take our cues from Jesus, we will begin there. We will give, serve, and love first, just like the EMTs who rescued Garrett all those years ago.

Perhaps, occasionally, the United States Congress should kick off a new session with a good ol' fashioned foot washing. It would require a lot of time. It would require a lot of humility. It would be mutual submission on the grandest scale imaginable. It would serve as a national reminder of our shared humanity—a reminder that every human being has far more in common with every other human being than not. Compared to what we have in common, our differences are miniscule.

Then again, perhaps we—the body of Christ—should go first.

After all, Jesus said *we* are the light of the world, not the US Congress. We are a city on a hill, not the United States of America. We are the salt of the earth. We are the body of Christ. The hands and feet of Jesus. Jesus, who did not come to be served but to serve and give his life as a ransom for many. Jesus, who refused to be appropriated by a party so he could address the hearts of people in both parties. Jesus, who stopped to listen, paused to heal, and gave his life for the very men who took it.

Jesus who lost.

Jesus who won.

So let's be quick to listen, slow to speak. Let's *not* keep our distance. Let's take our law-of-Christ informed consciences with us to the ballot box. Let's lead the way in acknowledging that there are no perfect solutions that involve people because people are involved in both the problems and the solutions. Let's love our enemies. Let's go out of our way to serve those who have arrived at different conclusions and embrace different solutions.

Let's be kind yet willing to call out unkindness in our party of choice, especially when it hurts or dehumanizes others. Let's be honest and willing to call out dishonesty when it undermines someone's dignity.

Let's not settle for being law-abiding citizens or patriotic Americans. We're called to something higher than that. More demanding than that. We're Jesus followers. So let's take up our crosses and follow. Let's do everything without grumbling or arguing so that we may become blameless and pure, children of God without fault in a warped and crooked generation.[17] Let's "shine among them like stars in the sky."[18] And let's do it in such a way that they see our good works and glorify our Father in heaven![19]

Let's live, love, and lead in such a way that we, the *ekklesia* of Jesus, regain the moral high ground and can serve as the conscience of our nation. Let's do what's just, not what we can justify. Let's do what's responsible, not what's permissible. Let's do what's moral, not what's modeled.

Let's stop trying to win.

Let's forsake our fear of losing.

Let's fix our eyes and our lives on Jesus.

Who, being in very nature God,
    did not consider equality with God something
        to be used to his own advantage;
rather, he made himself nothing
    by taking the very nature of a servant,
    being made in human likeness.

And being found in appearance as a man,
 he humbled himself
  by becoming obedient to death—
   even death on a cross!

Therefore God exalted him to the highest place
 and gave him the name that is above
  every name,
that at the name of Jesus every knee should bow,
 in heaven and on earth and under the earth,
and every tongue acknowledge that Jesus Christ
  is Lord,
  to the glory of God the Father.[20]

That's the win.

That's what will be celebrated when the clock runs out and the game ends.

NOTES

Introduction

1. Scott Galloway, "Scott Galloway on What to Expect in a Post-Pandemic World," Fast Company, July 1, 2021, https://www.fastcompany.com/90646334/scott-galloway-on-what-to-expect-in-a-post-pandemic-world.
2. See Philippians 2:14–15.
3. Matthew 5:16.
4. 1 Corinthians 12:27, italics added.
5. 1 Corinthians 12:24–25.
6. 1 Corinthians 12:25–26, italics added.

Chapter 1: Battle of the Buckets

1. Craig S. Keener, *Acts: An Exegetical Commentary, Volume 2, 3:1–14:28* (Grand Rapids: Baker Academic, 2012), Kindle, Acts 11:26.
2. See Acts 26:28.
3. 1 Corinthians 9:19, italics added.
4. 1 Corinthians 9:20–21.
5. 1 Corinthians 9:22.
6. 1 Corinthians 9:22.
7. 1 Corinthians 9:22, italics added.
8. Acts 17:30, italics added.
9. Galatians 3:28.
10. 1 Corinthians 9:22–23, italics added.
11. Matthew 28:20, italics added.
12. See 1 Corinthians 9:22.
13. Timothy Keller, "Justice in the Bible," Life in the Gospel, accessed November 29, 2021, https://quarterly.gospelinlife.com/justice-in-the-bible/.

14. See John 17.
15. See Mark 1:15.

Chapter 2: Culture War Christianity

1. "Reimagining Rights and Responsibilities in the United States," Harvard Kennedy School, accessed November 29, 2021, https://carrcenter.hks.harvard.edu/reimagining-rights-responsibilities-united-states.

2. "Reimagining Rights and Responsibilities in the United States," Harvard Kennedy School.

3. *Psychological Bulletin* 141, no. 6, 2015, cited in Kirk Waldroff, "Fear: A Powerful Motivator in Elections," American Psychological Association, October 13, 2020, https://www.apa.org/news/apa/2020/fear-motivator-elections.

4. Peter Wehner, "The Evangelical Church Is Breaking Apart," Atlantic, October 24, 2021, https://www.theatlantic.com/ideas/archive/2021/10/evangelical-trump-christians-politics/620469/.

5. Kristin Kobes Du Mez, quoted in Wehner, "The Evangelical Church Is Breaking Apart."

6. Mellissa Withers, "It's More Than Just Fight or Flight," *Psychology Today*, February 5, 2021, https://www.psychologytoday.com/us/blog/modern-day-slavery/202102/its-more-just-fight-or-flight.

7. James Davison Hunter in Jason Willick, "The Man Who Discovered 'Culture Wars,'" *Wall Street Journal*, May 25, 2018, https://www.wsj.com/articles/the-man-who-discovered-culture-wars-1527286035.

8. James Davison Hunter, *Culture Wars: The Struggle to Define America* (New York: Basic Books, 1992), 63.

9. David French, "How a Rising Religious Movement Rationalizes the Christian Grasp for Power," The Dispatch, February 28, 2021, https://frenchpress.thedispatch.com/p/how-a-rising-religious-movement-rationalizes.

10. French, "How a Rising Religious Movement Rationalizes the Christian Grasp for Power".

11. Jonathan Leeman, *How the Nations Rage: Rethinking Faith and Politics in a Divided Age* (Nashville: Nelson, 2018), 21.
12. Matthew 28:19.
13. Matthew 28:20.
14. John 15:12.
15. John 15:14.
16. Ed Stetzer, *Christians in the Age of Outrage: How to Bring Our Best When the World Is at Its Worst* (Carol Stream, IL: Tyndale, 2018), 105.
17. Matthew 6:24.
18. Matthew 6:24, italics added.
19. Acts 15:19, italics added.
20. Russell Moore, "Why the Church Is Losing the Next Generation," Moore to the Point, accessed November 29, 2021, http://createsend.com/t/r-6C1451630A966B6D2540EF23F30FEDED.
21. Robert P. Jones et al., *Exodus: Why Americans are Leaving Religion—And Why They're Unlikely to Come Back*, Public Religion Research Institute, September 22, 2016, https://www.prri.org/wp-content/uploads/2016/09/PRRI-RNS-Unaffiliated-Report.pdf.

Chapter 3: Canceled

1. "Megachurch Pastor: Worship Services Are Not Essential," CNN, July 15, 2020, https://www.cnn.com/videos/us/2020/07/15/megachurch-pastor-andy-stanley-suspends-worship-services-covid-19-atlanta-bts-nr-vpx.cnn.
2. Dictionary.com, s.v. "cancel culture (*n.*)," accessed October 26, 2021, https://www.dictionary.com/browse/cancel-culture.
3. Brooke Kato, "What Is Cancel Culture? Everything to Know about the Toxic Online Trend," *NYPost*, August 31, 2021, https://nypost.com/article/what-is-cancel-culture-breaking-down-the-toxic-online-trend/.
4. 1 Timothy 6:18.
5. 1 Corinthians 5:12, italics added.

6. 1 Corinthians 5:12.
7. 1 Corinthians 5:13.
8. Luke 15:20.
9. Luke 15:28–30.
10. Luke 15:31–32.

Chapter 4: Kingdoms in Conflict

1. Bart Ehrman, *The Triumph of Christianity: How a Forbidden Religion Swept the World* (New York: Simon & Schuster, 2018), 286, italics added.
2. Jordan Peterson, *12 Rules for Life: An Antidote to Chaos* (Toronto: Random House Canada, 2018), 186, italics added.
3. Peterson, *12 Rules for Life*, 187, italics added.
4. Michael Levin, "Natural Subordination, Aristotle on," *Philosophy* 72, no. 280 (1997): 241, italics added.
5. In John Dickson, *Bullies and Saints: An Honest Look at the Good and Evil of Christian History* (Grand Rapids: Zondervan, 2021), 34. Letter of Hilarion, Oxyrhynchus Papyri (ed. B. P. Grenfell and A. S. Hunt). 4:744. Readers can view the letter itself online, together with the above translation and some discussion, http://www.papyri.info/apis/toronto.apis.17/.
6. Peterson, *12 Rules for Life*, 187.
7. Didache, Early Christian Writings, accessed November 29, 2021, http://www.earlychristianwritings.com/text/didache-roberts.html.
8. Philip Yancey, *Vanishing Grace: Bringing Good News to a Deeply Divided World* (Grand Rapids: Zondervan, 2014), 171.
9. Yancey, *Vanishing Grace*, 171.
10. Yancey, *Vanishing Grace*, 171.
11. Matthew 3:2, italics added.
12. John 1:29, italics added.
13. Mark 1:14.
14. Mark 1:15.
15. Matthew 3:2, italics added.
16. Mark 1:15.

17. John 1:4–5, italics added.
18. See Matthew 5:9.
19. Ehrman, *The Triumph of Christianity*, 286, italics added.
20. Karen Armstrong, *Fields of Blood: Religion and the History of Violence* (New York: Knopf Doubleday, 2014), 149.

Chapter 5: On Brand

1. John 13:33.
2. John 13:34.
3. See Matthew 22:37–40.
4. See Luke 7:48–49 and Luke 5:21–22.
5. John 13:34.
6. John 13:34.
7. John 13:35, italics added.
8. John 13:35, italics added.
9. D. A. Carson, *Love in Hard Places* (Wheaton, IL: Crossway, 2002), 60–61.
10. Carson, *Love in Hard Places*, 61.
11. Carson, *Love in Hard Places*, 61.
12. John 13:34.
13. See John 13:15.
14. Matthew 28:18.
15. John 13:3, italics added.
16. John 13:4–5, italics added.
17. John 13:12–13.
18. John 13:14–18, italics added.
19. Matthew 4:19.
20. John 13:35.
21. See Rodney Stark's *The Triumph of Christianity*, Michael Walsh's *The Triumph of the Meek*, and Alvin J. Schmidt's *How Christianity Changed the World*.
22. This and the next several Pliny quotes from Pliny, *Letters* 10.96 (Radice, Loeb Classical Library 59), 285–91.
23. Tertullian, *Apologeticus* 40.2.
24. Genesis 1:1.

25. Pliny *Epistulae* 10.96–7.
26. Pliny *Epistulae* 10.96–7.
27. Pliny *Epistulae* 10.96–7, italics added.
28. Pliny *Epistulae* 10.96–7.
29. Pliny *Epistulae* 10.96–7.
30. Luke 23:4.
31. 1 Thessalonians 4:11–12.
32. Pliny *Epistulae* 10.96–7.
33. Pliny *Epistulae* 10.96–7.
34. Pliny *Epistulae* 10.96–7, italics added.
35. Pliny *Epistulae* 10.96–7.
36. John 13:34–35.

Chapter 6: One for the Win

1. "Partisan Antipathy: More Intense, More Personal," Pew Research Center, October 10, 2019, https://www.pew research.org/politics/2019/10/10/partisan-antipathy-more -intense-more-personal/.
2. Harry Enten, "Statistically, Democrats and Republicans Hate Each Other More than Ever," CNN, November 20, 2021, https://www.cnn.com/2021/11/20/politics/democrat -republican-hate-tribalism/index.html.
3. Justin Giboney (@JustinEGiboney), "One ugly reality . . ." Twitter, June 8, 2021, 8:15 a.m., https://twitter.com/JustinE Giboney/status/1402237801924550664.
4. See James 1:19.
5. Matthew 5:43.
6. Matthew 5:44.
7. Matthew 5:45, italics added.
8. Matthew 5:46, italics added.
9. Matthew 5:15–16, italics added.
10. John 17:20.
11. John 17:1.
12. John 17:2.
13. John 17:3.

14. John 17:4, italics added.
15. John 17:11, italics added.
16. John 17:18.
17. John 17:20, italics added.
18. John 17:20, italics added.
19. John 17:20–21, italics added.
20. John 17:21, italics added.
21. Galatians 5:15.
22. John 17:21, italics added.
23. John 17:21, italics added.
24. Chuck Mingo, Courageous Love: Healing Our Racial Divide Webinar, Right Now Media, https://www.rightnowmedia .org/webinar/chuck-mingo-courageous-love.
25. Matthew 16:18.

Chapter 7: The Supper of God

1. Ephesians 6:12, italics added.
2. See Ephesians 6:11.
3. See Matthew 12:25.
4. Colossians 4:5.
5. Colossians 4:6.
6. Acts 15:19.
7. 1 Corinthians 9:19–23.
8. Colossians 2:17, italics added.
9. John 14:8.
10. John 14:8–9.
11. See 1 Corinthians 5:12.
12. Philippians 2:7–8.
13. Revelation 19:11, italics added.
14. Revelation 19:12–13.
15. Revelation 19:14–15.
16. Revelation 19:15–16.
17. Revelation 19:17, italics added.
18. Revelation 19:18, italics added.
19. Revelation 19:19–21, italics added.

20. Urban II, speech at Council of Clermont, 1095, https://source books.fordham.edu/source/urban2-fulcher.asp.
21. John Dickson, *Bullies and Saints: An Honest Look at the Good and Evil of Christian History* (Grand Rapids: Zondervan, 2021), 52.

Chapter 8: Inquisitor in Chief

1. Acts 7:60.
2. Acts 8:1, italics added.
3. Luke 23:33.
4. Acts 8:1–2.
5. Acts 8:3, italics added.
6. Acts 8:3, italics added.
7. Acts 22:4, italics added.
8. Acts 22:3, italics added.
9. Philippians 3:5–6, italics added.
10. Galatians 1:13–14.
11. Deuteronomy 13:6, 8–10.
12. Acts 9:23–24.
13. Acts 9:26.
14. Acts 23:10.
15. Acts 23:12–13.
16. Acts 23:14–15.
17. Romans 5:10.
18. Galatians 1:6–7.
19. Galatians 1:8.
20. Galatians 1:9.
21. Galatians 5:2.
22. Galatians 5:2–3.
23. See Hebrews 8:13.
24. Galatians 5:9.
25. Galatians 5:12.
26. Galatians 5:12.
27. Philip Yancey, *Vanishing Grace: Bringing Good News to a Deeply Divided World* (Grand Rapids: Zondervan, 2014), 171.

28. Matthew 28:18.
29. John 14:9.
30. See Colossians 2:17.
31. Jeremiah 29:11.
32. Matthew 28:20.
33. Philippians 3:7–11.
34. Philippians 3:12–14, italics added.

Chapter 9: Apply Only as Directed

1. See Philippians 2:12.
2. See James 2:17.
3. James 2:14, italics added.
4. Philippians 2:15, italics added.
5. Matthew 5:16.
6. "Justice Department Announces Multi-Million Dollar Civil Settlement in Principle in Mother Emanuel Charleston Church Mass Shooting," U.S. Department of Justice, October 28, 2021, https://www.justice.gov/opa/pr/justice -department-announces-multi-million-dollar-civil-settlement -principle-mother-emanuel.
7. "Families Speak to Dylann Roof: 'We Have No Room for Hate,'" *Los Angeles Times*, June 19, 2015, https://www .latimes.com/nation/ct-families-forgive-charleston-church -shooting-suspect-20150619-story.html.
8. "Families Speak to Dylann Roof."
9. "Families Speak to Dylann Roof."
10. Rachael J. Denhollander, "I Was the First Woman to Publicly Accuse Gymnastics Doctor Larry Nassar. But I Was Also Abused in My Own Church," *Washington Post*, September, 9, 2019, https://www.washingtonpost.com/religion/2019/09 /09/i-was-first-woman-publicly-accuse-gymnastics-doctor -larry-nassar-i-was-also-abused-my-own-church/.
11. "Larry Nassar Case: USA Gymnastics Doctor 'Abused 265 Girls,'" *BBC News*, January 31, 2018, https://www.bbc.com /news/world-us-canada-42894833.

12. "Read: Biles, Maroney, Raisman and Nichols Opening Statements before Congress," *CNN*, September 16, 2021, https://www.cnn.com/2021/09/15/politics/read-usa-gymnasts-testimony/index.html.

13. This and the next three quotes are from "Read Rachael Denhollander's Full Victim Impact Statement about Larry Nassar," *CNN*, January 30, 2018, https://www.cnn.com/2018/01/24/us/rachael-denhollander-full-statement/index.html.

14. Philippians 2:15.

15. See Acts 25:11.

16. See Romans 13:1–7.

17. Romans 13:4.

18. Jonathan Leeman, *How the Nations Rage: Rethinking Faith and Politics in a Divided Age* (Nashville: Nelson, 2018), 69.

19. Leeman, *How the Nations Rage*, 64.

20. Matthew 5:16, italics added.

21. See 1 Peter 2:12.

22. See 1 Peter 2:15.

23. Mark 10:42.

24. Four words in our English text. Six words in the Greek text.

25. Mark 10:43.

26. Mark 10:43.

27. Mark 10:43–44.

28. Mark 10:45.

29. Mark 14:50.

30. This and the next two quotes are from Mark 8:35.

31. Mark 8:36.

32. Mark 8:34.

33. John 15:12.

34. Galatians 6:2.

35. Galatians 6:2, italics added.

36. Ephesians 4:31–32.

37. Ephesians 4:32.

38. Russell Moore, "Why Unhealthy People Crave Controversy," The Gospel Coalition, September 9, 2020, https://www.

thegospelcoalition.org/article/unhealthy-people-crave
-controversy/.

39. Ephesians 5:1–2, italics added.
40. Ephesians 5:2, italics added.
41. Russell Moore, "Losing Our Religion," Russell Moore, April 15, 2021, https://www.russellmoore.com/2021/04/15 /losing-our-religion/.
42. John 19:10, my translation from Greek text.
43. Jesus answered, "You would have no power over me if it were not given to you from above" (John 19:11).

Chapter 10: Most Important Now

1. Dinnertime conversation, October 9, 2021.
2. Hebrews 12:1.
3. Hebrews 12:1.
4. Hebrews 12:2.
5. Dinnertime conversation, October 9, 2021.
6. See Matthew 15:15–22.
7. John 8:11.
8. Matthew 15:18, italics added.
9. Matthew 15:19.
10. Matthew 15:20.
11. Aleksandr Solzhenitsyn, *The Gulag Archipelago*, 1918–1956.
12. John 1:17.
13. John 14:9.
14. This and the next four quotes are from John 13:12–17, italics added.
15. See Galatians 6:2.
16. John 13:35.
17. See Philippians 2:14–15.
18. Philippians 2:15.
19. See Matthew 5:16.
20. Philippians 2:6–11.

ABOUT THE AUTHOR

Communicator, author, and pastor Andy Stanley founded Atlanta-based North Point Ministries (NPM) in 1995. Today, NPM consists of eight churches in the Atlanta area and a network of 180 churches around the globe that collectively serve over 200,000 people weekly. A survey of US pastors in *Outreach* magazine identified Andy as one of the ten most influential living pastors in America.

Andy holds an undergraduate degree in journalism from Georgia State University and a master's degree from Dallas Theological Seminary. He is the author of more than 20 books, including *Better Decisions, Fewer Regrets*; *Irresistible; The New Rules for Love, Sex & Dating; How to Be Rich; Deep & Wide; Enemies of the Heart; When Work & Family Collide;* and *Visioneering.*

Your Move with Andy Stanley premiered on NBC after *Saturday Night Live* in 2012 and on CBS after *The Late Late Show with James Corden* in 2017, giving Andy an even wider audience with which to share his culturally relevant, practical insights for life and leadership. Currently, over

10 million messages are consumed each month through television, YouTube, and podcasts, underscoring Andy's impact not only as a communicator but also as an influencer of culture.

Nothing is as personal as his passion for engaging with live audiences, which he has pursued for over three decades at leadership events around the world. In high demand, he speaks at various annual events before audiences of both church and organizational leaders.

"I cannot fill their cups," he often says of the opportunity to impact leaders in business and in ministry, "but I have a responsibility to empty mine."

Andy and his wife, Sandra, have three grown children and live near Atlanta.

Once upon a time there existed a version of our faith worth the world found irresistible.

In this book and six-session study, Andy Stanley shows us how Jesus' arrival signaled that the Old Testament was fulfilled and its laws reduced to a single verb—love—to be applied to God, neighbor, and enemy. So, what is required if we want to follow Jesus' example and radically love the people around us? We almost always know the answer. The hard part is actually doing what love requires.

Rather than working harder to make Christianity more interesting, we need to recover what once made faith in Jesus irresistible to the world.

Book	Study Guide	DVD
9780310536970	9780310100492	9780310100515

Available now at your favorite bookstore,
or streaming video on StudyGateway.com.

Deep & Wide

Andy Stanley

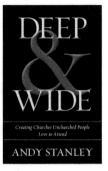

Andy Stanley's bestselling and award-winning vision for the local church is now available in softcover. New bonus content includes a study guide, church staff helps, and an interview with Andy on the most frequently asked questions about *Deep and Wide*.

With surprising candor and transparency, pastor Andy Stanley explains how one of America's largest churches began with a high-profile divorce and a church split.

But that's just the beginning...

Deep and Wide provides church leaders with an in-depth look into North Point Community Church and its strategy for creating churches unchurched people absolutely love to attend.

Going Deep & Wide

A Companion Guide for Churches and Leaders

Andy Stanley

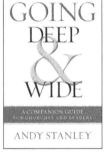

Every Sunday people walk into your church and decide if they will return the following week before the preacher even opens his mouth. Many of those people don't know what to make of Jesus. They're hesitant to be in church. They're not sure they belong. But over and over in the pages of Scripture, we see something extraordinary.

People who were nothing like Jesus liked Jesus.

Shouldn't that be true of the church as well?

In *Going Deep and Wide*, Andy Stanley lays out a blueprint and offers practical steps to help you turn up the irresistible in your church. Each section includes discussion materials that walk you deeper into the content of *Deep and Wide* and invite conversations about how to apply what you've learned.

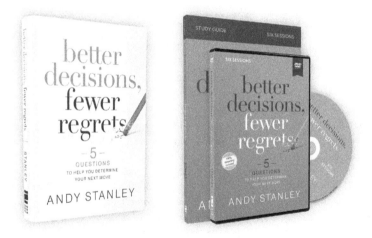

CPSIA information can be obtained
at www.ICGtesting.com
Printed in the USA
BVHW030021280722
643196BV00020B/227

9 780310 138921

2

3

POSEY

Passion: Acting

Color: Pink

Pet: Floofy gray cat

Fave magical creature: Unicorn

Ultra-Super-Power:
UltraSparkle Bracelet

Personal Motto:
Born to shine!!!

ANNA

Passion: Gymnastics

Color: Turquoise

Pet: Golden Labrador Retriever

Fave magical creature: Fairy

Ultra-Super Power: Ultra-Boost!

Personal Motto:
Girls Run the World...and the Galaxy

4

LYRIC

Passion: Music

Color: Purple

Pet: Hedgehog

Fave magical creature:
Dragon

Ultra-Super-Power:
Ultra-Sonic!

Personal Motto: Girls rock!

SKY

Passion: Tech

Color: Green

Pet: She's getting a new puppy!
Maybe by the end of this book!

Fave magical creature: Griffin

Ultra-Super-Power:
Ultra-Brainz!

Personal Motto:
Problem? Problem solved!

7

Captain Bardo Babu
"BOB"

Secret Dream:
To become a spy

Signature Color: Red

Signature Item:
His imagination

Personal Motto:
I'll stick by your side

Lieutenant Cruzob Shlunk
"Shlunk"

Secret Dream: Endless naps

Signature Color: Yellow

Signature Item:
Blanky

Personal Motto:
Just chillin'

Sergeant Lo-Jane
"JANE"

Secret Dream:
To be a super star!

Signature Color:
Rainbow

Signature Item:

Personal Motto: Hugs and Squishes!

Airman Darval Loofah
"LOUIE"

Secret Dream:
To have his own cooking show

Signature Color: Orange

Signature Item: TACO!

Personal Motto:
Want tacos!

10

Izzy giggles a lot!

Fia is a fast crawler!

Toño loves his binky!

Boondoggle likes to cuddle!

FOR THE FIRST TIME IN A MILLENNIUM...

PALIDORIA IS HOSTING THE ALL-UNIVERSE DANCE COMPETITION:

THE GALAXY GLAM-JAM!

DANCE TEAMS FROM ALL OVER HAVE TRAVELED LIGHT YEARS...

TO COMPETE FOR THE HONOR OF TAKING THE GLAM-JAM TROPHY BACK TO THEIR HOME PLANET.

DIFFERENT WORLDS, ALL COMING TOGETHER.

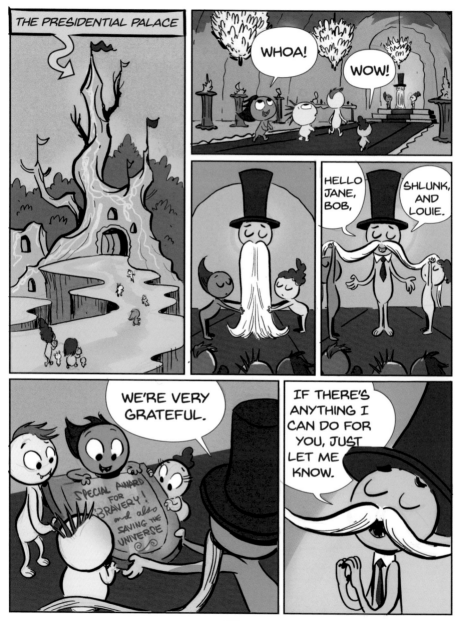

THE PRESIDENTIAL PALACE

WHOA!

WOW!

HELLO JANE, BOB,

SHLUNK, AND LOUIE.

WE'RE VERY GRATEFUL.

SPECIAL AWARD FOR BRAVERY! and also SAVING THE UNIVERSE

IF THERE'S ANYTHING I CAN DO FOR YOU, JUST LET ME KNOW.

14

16

17

18

19

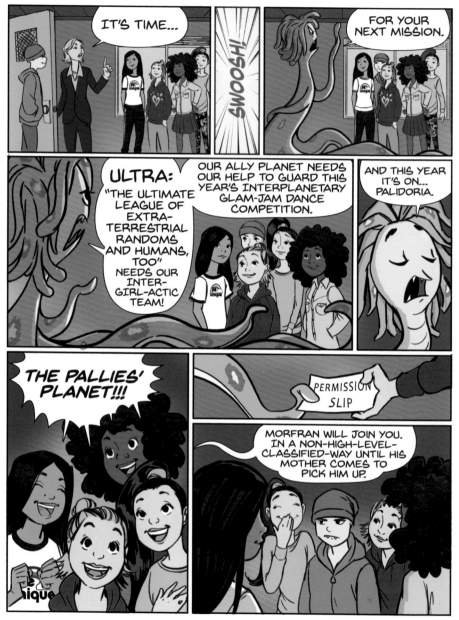

21

22

23

25

26

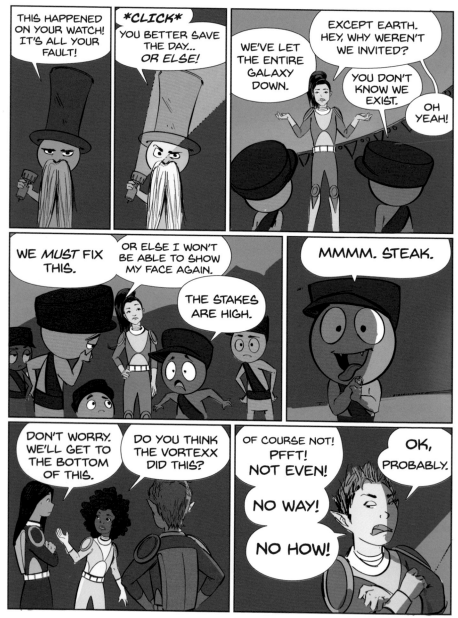

28

YES, THAT'S RIGHT-- LEGEND HAS IT THAT FOUR ANCIENTS SET OUT TO FIND **THE SHARD OF INFINITE KINDNESS** TO SHARE WITH EVERY LIVING BEING. BUT, AFTER A MILLENNIA OF SEARCHING THEY FOUND NOTHING. THE ANCIENTS DID NOT WANT THEIR JOURNEY TO GO FOR NAUGHT, SO THEY HAD A BRILLIANT IDEA. THEY CREATED AN ENORMOUS MACHINE CALLED **THE BEAT,** WHICH PROJECTS A GUIDING LIGHT TO ALL CORNERS OF THE GALAXY. THE LIGHT NOT ONLY PROVIDES A PATHWAY FOR GOOD, BUT ALSO SHINES A LIGHT ON THE BAD, MEANING...

...IF THERE IS NO LIGHT THEN EVIL CAN MOVE THROUGHOUT THE GALAXY - UNDETECTED.

WE HAVE TO GO TO THE CORE!

NOT A FAN OF SMALL SPACES.

NOT A FAN OF PALIWOGGLES.

WHAT ARE PALI-WOGGLES?

34

THERE ARE *FIVE!*

ONCE YOU FIND THEM, YOU CAN MOVE ON!

I KNOW THIS GAME! CHOOSE A WORD FOR EACH PART OF SPEECH SPECIFIED.

READ THE STORY ON THE NEXT PAGE OUT LOUD, FILLING YOUR WORDS IN THE BLANKS.

ADJECTIVE: _____

PART OF BODY: _____

ANIMAL: _____

CARTOON CHARACTER: _____

COLOR: _____

EXCLAMATION: _____

ADJECTIVE: _____

NUMBER: _____

PART OF BODY: _____

SUPER POWER: _____

THE MYSTERY OF THE PALIWOGGLES

THE PALIWOGGLES ARE RUMORED TO HAVE
_____ [ADJECTIVE] _____ [PART OF BODY].
THEY ARE _____ [NUMBER] FEET TALL.
SOME SAY THEY LOOK LIKE A MASHUP OF A _____
[ANIMAL] AND _____ [CARTOON CHARACTER].
THEY MIGHT BE _____ [COLOR].
_____! [EXCLAMATION] !
THAT COULD BE REALLY SCARY.

THEY HAVE LIVED INSIDE THE PLANET
FOR _____ [NUMBER] YEARS.

ACCORDING TO MYTHOLOGY, LOOKING INTO THEIR
_____ [PART OF BODY] COULD TURN YOU INTO STONE!
THEY ARE SUPPOSED TO HAVE THE MAGICAL POWER OF
_____ [SUPER POWER].

HOWEVER, SINCE NOBODY BUT THE ANCIENTS HAVE EVER SEEN
THEM, ALL OR NONE OF THIS COULD BE TRUE! WE MAY NEVER
FIND OUT.... OR WILL WE?

WE DID IT!
WE CAN
MOVE ON!

44

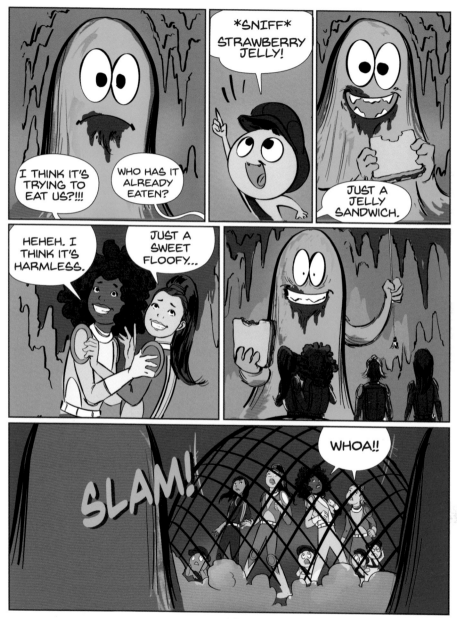

45

46

47

48

49

50

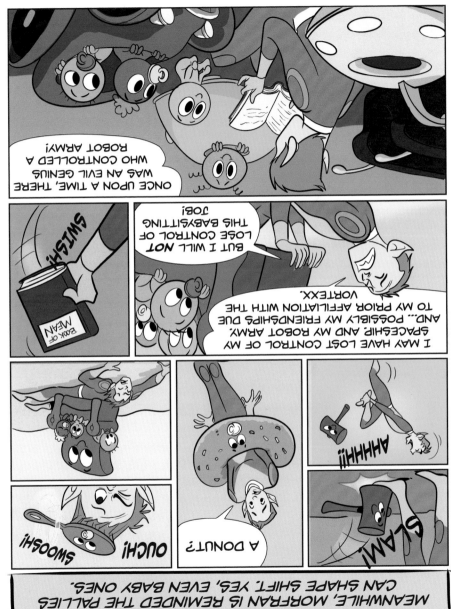

57

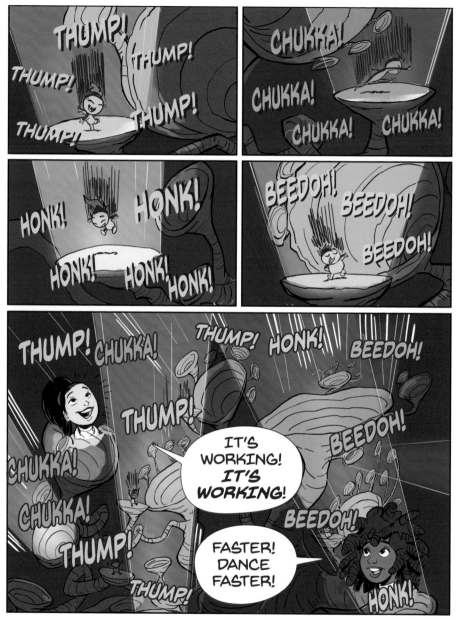

63

65

68

69

70

71

74

75

78

79

82

83

84

85

87

89

SO IN THE END, THE PALIDORIANS WERE WINNERS, TOO. THEY HOSTED AN AWESOME GLAM-JAM AND BROUGHT EVERYONE TOGETHER "HAPALLIE" EVER AFTER.

THE CREATORS

Author
Julia DeVillers is the author of books including TRADING FACES and THE AUDITION with Maddie Ziegler. Her book became the Disney Channel Original Movie READ IT AND WEEP. She is the author of ULTRASQUAD and ULTRASQUAD: UNDER THE STRANGEBOW.

Co-Author
R.R. Wells is a writer, producer, and director of animated short films. R.R. is the co-author of ULTRASQUAD and ULTRASQUAD: UNDER THE STRANGEBOW.

Illustrator
Rafael Rosado is the illustrator and co-creator of the graphic novel series GIANTS BEWARE, MONSTERS BEWARE, and DRAGONS BEWARE. He is currently a storyboard artist for Warner Brothers, Disney, and Cartoon Network.

Colorist: John Novak
Production Manager/Letterer: Kylie Lovsey
Inker/Penciler: Will Rosado
Inker/Penciler: Josh Tufts
Inker/Penciler: Dave Alvarez
Inker/Penciler: Dan Root
Assistant Visual Designer: Jay Graham
3D Artist: Patrick Danber
Producer: Jeremy Hughes
Executive Producer: Joe Niedecken
Cover Designer: Kylie Lovsey

Special thanks to Lece Lohr, Sara Tervo, Kendra Stokes, Traci Graziani, Lizzy Maurer, and Meghan Kerr!!!

MAKE SURE TO KEEP UP WITH ALL THINGS ULTRASQUAD AT YOUR NEAREST JUSTICE STORE!

**

For information regarding the CPSIA on this printed material, call: (203) 595-3636 and provide reference #RICH - 826015.

Printed in the United States of America.

First edition.

ISBN-978-1-7327030-0-1